Gastronomic
DICTIONARY

French - English

Thomas Harmsworth

Thomas Harmsworth's
Gastronomic Dictionary
French-English
THOMAS HARMSWORTH PUBLISHING COMPANY

© 2003 Thomas Harmsworth Publishing Company
First Published 2003
Reprinted 2003, 2005, 2010

The publisher regrets that it can accept no responsibility for any errors or omissions
within this publication, or for any expenses or loss thereby caused.

A few words are included in this dictionary which are asserted to be proprietary names.
The presence or absence of such names should not be considered to affect the legal
status of any such names or trade marks.

British Library Cataloguing-in-Publication Data. A catalogue record of this book is
available from the British Library.

In the same series:
Spanish-English
Italian-English
Portuguese-English

ISBN 978-0-948807-53-4
ISSN 1741-3370

Printed in Great Britain by
Creeds the Printers

Introduction

French is the language of food. But there can be few outside France who would be able to read a french menu without difficulty. Even to the French, some of the dishes, or ingredients, are unfamiliar and need explanation from the waiter. *Gastronomic Dictionary* is designed to help the diner over a large number of the pitfalls.

Saint-amour, saint-honoré, saint-mandé, saint-paulin, saint-pierre. What are they? A wine, a patisserie, a garnish, a cheese, a fish! And cheeses and wines are so often key ingredients in a dish.

This is not a dictionary of wine. But wines are often used in, and used to describe, local dishes. These wines will be unfamiliar to most travellers. They are therefore listed, simply to identify them as wines: not to describe the colour, quality or type of grape. By the same token, the internationally renowned wines (e.g. Nuits-St-Georges) are not necessarily listed, as being sufficiently well-known to the diner. Also the lesser wines (mainly clarets) which start with the word 'Château' are not listed as being self-evidently wines.

This is not a dictionary of cheeses, either. But here again, it is difficult for the traveller to know whether the word on the menu is indeed a cheese. The French name for it is therefore simply identified as a cheese, and whether it is of goat, ewe or cow's milk.

Gastronomic Dictionary is not a dictionary which will explain menu entries in a chinese, indian, kosher or other specialising restaurant, but there are nevertheless a few terms that might be found in such establishments.

Many French culinary terms are steeped in history, and are often too general for short and precise definitions. An example of this is

Bagration, which applies to a variety of dishes (eggs, fish soup, meat soup, salad, timbales &c) which have no common denominator, other than that they were dishes originally designed by the famous French late 18th century chef, Carême, to please Princess Bagration (see the delightful *Larousse Gastronomique).* In such cases, because the cooking method concerned may apply to radically different ingredients, it is best to ascertain from the waiter what to expect! French chefs used to vie with each other for the honour of having a dish named after them. Thus many preparations are named after their inventor, and a description may relate to several different basic ingredients. Dishes are also very often named after heroes in opera or plays, and opera themselves, or a famous actor or actress.

The Dictionary also covers words not immediately relevant to the dining-room or kitchen. Some restaurants have a few rooms for overnight accommodation. *Gastronomic Dictionary* therefore includes a few very basic definitions that really relate to hotel travel.

Other than if the word is largely a description of the way a dish is presented (e.g. crown-shaped patisserie), definitions do not include presentation but only enough of the basic ingredients to indicate the character of the dish. Likewise, definitions do not expressly cover the preparation of ingredients which, in themselves, may then become a main ingredient.

In France beef, lamb, pork, veal &c. is cut by butchers in different ways to in England. The French method tends to be more detailed, with the effect that some of the French cuts do not have precise English translations. Also, ingredients of dishes vary: some french dishes do not have an english synonym, only a descriptive string of words.

The French tend to use lower case initial letters for proper nouns, (e.g. crème dieppoise for Dieppe creamed sauce), which may make comprehension by tourists difficult, particularly if not familiar with French regions or lesser vineyards. We have, largely, used lower-case lettering too.

To denote the feminine of an adjective, it is usual to add 'e' as an ending to the masculine word; where it is thought helpful, the feminine ending is added in brackets after the masculine headword.

On 16th February, 1755, Fanny Burney's father, Charles Burney, wrote to the famous 'Dictionary' Johnson. Burney asked Dr Johnson to supply him with 6 copies of his *Dictionary of the English Language.* Johnson apologised for not being able to supply them personally, and charmingly wrote: 'When you have leisure to think again upon me, let me be favoured with another letter, and another yet, when you have looked into my Dictionary. If you find faults, I shall endeavour to mend them: if you find none, I shall think you blinded by kind partiality: but to have made you partial in his favour will very much gratify the ambition of, Sir, Your most obliged And most humble servant, SAM JOHNSON.'

We say the same.

Bon Appétit!
Enjoy your Meal!

A

abaisse *nf* rolled pastry

abats *nfpl* giblets, offal

abattis *nmpl* giblets

abattoir *nm* abattoir

abattre *vt* (of animal) to kill, to slaughter

abeille *nf* bee

abignardes (abegnardes) *nmpl* goose liver/tripe cooked in its blood

abîmer (s') *vi* to spoil; (of fruit) to bruise

able *nm* freshwater fish: leucaspius delineatus: sunbleak

ablette *nf* freshwater fish: bleak

abondance *nf* abundance, plenty; cow's milk cheese

abordable *a* affordable

aboukir *nm* chestnut-creamed sponge cake

abricot *nm* apricot; **~ de saint-domingue** sapodilla fruit

absinthe *nf* absinth, wormwood liqueur

abstinence *nf* abstinence

abyssal *a* pelagic, deep-sea, open-sea

acalorique *a* calory-free

accolade *nf* combination

accompagnement *nm* accompaniment, garnish, trimmings; **plat d'~** side-dish

accompagner *vt* to accompany, to go with

accro *nm/f* chocaholic

acéré *a* (of blade) sharp

acetomel *nm* vinegar/honey mix

achar (achard) *nm* spicy fruit/vegetable pickle

ache *nf* wild celery, water parsley; **~ de montagne** lovage

achigan (achigon) *nm* black bass

acide *a* sour

acidité *nf* acidity

acidulé *a* slightly acid; (of sweet) acid drop

acompte *nm* deposit

acra (akra) *nf* spiced puréed fish or vegetable fritter

âcre *a* (of taste) rough, sharp

additif *nm* additive

addition *nf* bill

additionné *a* added

adipeux (euse) *a* adipose; of animal fat

adoucir *vt* to sweeten

advocaat *nm* advocaat, egg-yolk liqueur

aegle *nm* citrus fruit

aéroport *nm* airport

affilé *a* (of knife) sharp

affiler *vt* (of knife) to sharpen

affiné *a* (of cheese) mature

affûté *a* (of knife) sharp

africaine (à l') *a* potato/2 vegetables-garnished

agapes *nfpl* feast, banquet

agar-agar (agar) *nm* agar-agar, stabilising/thickening agent

agaric *nm* agaric, capped mushroom

agave *nm* agave, tequila-producing plant

aggloméré *nm* (of charcoal) briquette

agiter *vt* (of bottle) to shake

agneau (agnelle) *nm* lamb

agnelet *nm* young lamb

Agnès Sorel *a* mushroom/chicken/tongue-garnished

agraz *nm* almond/verjuice sorbet

agréable *a* pleasant

agricole *a* agricultural; **politique ~ commune** Common Agricultural Policy

agrume *nm* citrus fruit

aguardiente *nf* eau-de-vie, marc

aïda *a* paprika/mornay sauce/spinach-ed

aide de cuisine *nm/f* kitchen hand

aigle de mer (raie-aigle) *nm* sea fish: eagle ray

aiglefin (églefin) *nm* haddock

aïgo boulido *nf* garlic soup

aigre *a* sour, (of wine) acid; **crème ~** sour cream

aigre-doux *a* sweet and sour

aiguière *nf* ewer, wide-mouthed jug

aiguillat *nm* sea fish: spurdog fish

aiguille *nf* needle; **~ voyeuse de mer rouge** sea fish: garfish variety

aiguillette *nf* aiguillette; strip of breast; top of rump

aiguiser *vt* (of knife) to sharpen; (of appetite) to whet

aiguisoir *nm* (of knife) sharpener, steel

ail (aulx *pl)* *nm* garlic

aile *nf* wing; (of chicken) white meat

aileron *nm* wing; **~ de requin** shark wing

aillade *nf* garlic sauce

aillée *nf* almond/garlic/breadcrumb condiment

ailler *vt* to garlic

ailloli, aïoli *nm* aïoli, garlic mayonnaise

air (en plein) *nm* alfresco

airelle *nf* bilberry, blueberry, whortleberry, huckleberry; **~ rouge** cranberry

albumen *nm* albumen, egg-white

alcalin *a* alkaline

alevin *nm* alevin; reared young

fish *(esp* salmon)

Alexandra *nf* chocolate liqueur cocktail; chocolate gateau; (of food) *a* Alexandra, asparagus/ truffle/sauce-garnished

algérienne (à l') *a* Algérienne, fried sweet-potato/tomato/ garlic-garnished

algue *nf* seaweed

algues *nm* (of gateau) laverbread

alica *nm* semolina

aligot *nf* cheese/garlic potato

aligoté *nm* white burgundy; grape variety

aliment *nm* food

alimentation *nf* diet, feeding, nourishment

alimenter *vt* to feed

allaitement *nm* suckling

alléchant *a* mouth-watering

allégé *a* (of milk, cheese) low-fat

allemande (à l') *a* allemande, white-sauced

allergique à *a* allergic to

alliacé *a* alliaceous, having garlic/onion smell

alliance *nf* blend

allonger *vt* to spin out; (of soup &c) to thin down

allumette *nf* match; flaky pastry stick; cheese straw; chip

alose *nf* shad

alouette *nf* lark

aloyau *nm* sirloin

alpage *nm* mountain pasture

alsacien (ienne) *a* Alsatian; sauerkraut/ham/bacon/

sausage-garnished

altérer (s') *vi* (of meat) to go off

amande *nf* almond, kernel; **pâte d'~(s)** marzipan; **~ de mer** small mollusc

amandine *nf* almond tart

amanite *nf* mushroom variety: grisette

amarante *nf* amaranth, Chinese spinach

amaretto *nf* amaretto, bitter almond liqueur

ambassadeur (drice) *a* ambassadeur (ambassadrice); duxelles-stuffed artichoke hearts/duchesse potato/ horseradish-garnished

ambre *nm* almond cream cake

ambré *a* ambre

ambre gris *nm* ambergris

ambroisie *nf* ambrosia, food for the gods

amer (ère) *a* bitter

américaine (à l') *a* with tomatoes/bacon

américano *nm* americano, lemon/vermouth cocktail

amidon *nm* (of food) starch

amincissant *a* (of diet) slimming

amiral (à l') *a* with Nantua-sauced shellfish/mushroom/ truffles

amollir *vt* (of butter &c) to soften

amoricaine (à l') *a* of Brittany; américaine dish with shrimp garnish

amour *nm* carp

amourette *nf* bone marrow

amuse-gueule (~ bouche)
nm appetizer; canapé;
scratching(s)

anacarde *nm* cashew nut

ananas *nm* pineapple

anchoïade (anchoyade) *nf*
anchovy paste

anchois *nm* anchovy

ancienne (à l') *a* onion/
mushroom-garnished fricassée

andalouse (à l') *a* (of meat,
soup) peppers/tomato/
aubergine/rice-garnished

andouille *nf* offal sausage

andouillette *nf* chitterlings; small
intestines

âne *nm* donkey, ass

aneth *nm* dill

ange de mer *nm* sea fish:
monkfish

angélique *nf* angelica

angelot *nm* group of Normandy
cheeses

anges à cheval *nmpl* angels on
horseback, grilled oysters on
bacon-ed toast

angevine (à l') *a* from Anjou;
cream/mushroom-sauced

anglais (e) (à l') *a* plain; (of
vegetables) boiled; (of beer)
bitter; **assiette ~e** variety of
cold meats; **petit déjeuner à
l'~e** cooked breakfast

anguille *nf* eel, **~ de roche**
conger eel

angusture (angostura) *nf*
angostura

animelles *nfpl* testicles

anis *nm* aniseed, anise

anisette *nf* anisette, aniseed
liqueur

anna *a* (of potatoes) anna,
sliced/casseroled

anneau *nm* (of can, tin) ring-pull

annette *a* (of potatoes) annette,
sliced-in-strips/casseroled

anniversaire *nm* anniversary,
birthday; **gâteau d' ~** birthday
cake

annuaire *nm* yearbook

annuler *vt* (of table reservation)
to cancel

anon *nm* sea fish: haddock

anone *nf* custard apple

antalgique *nm* analgesic

antiadhésif (ive) *a* non-stick

antibes (d') *a* of Antibes; **melon
d'~** honeydew melon

antiboise (à l') *a* of Antibes;
small-fish/garlic/tomato-
garnished

antillaise (à l') *a* of the Antilles;
(of poultry/fish) vegetable
or fruit sauce-coated rice-
garnished; (of fruit desserts)
with rum

antilope *nf* antelope

antipasto *nm* antipasto, hors
d'oeuvre

anversoise (à l') *a* of Antwerp;
hop shoot-garnished

apaiser *vt* (of hunger/ thirst) to
assuage

apéritif (apéro) *nm* aperitif,
pre-meal drink; **~ de la maison**
house aperitif

aphrodisiaque *nm* aphrodisiac

aplatir *vt* to flatten

appareil *nm* apparatus; prepared ingredients

appâté *a* fattened-up

appellation *nf* (of origin) legal name denoting a standard

appenzel *nm* gruyère-like cow's milk cheese

appétit *nm* appetite; garlic/shallots &c as culinary enhancements

apprêt *nm* dressing; culinary process

apprêter *vt* (of food) to prepare

approvisionnement *nm* (of food) supply, provisionment

âpre *a* pungent, rough, sharp

aquarium *nf* fishtank

aquavit *nm* aquavit, flavoured potato/starch spirit

arabica *nm* arabica; coffee bean

arachide *nf* peanut, groundnut, monkey nut

arack (arak) *nm* arrack (arak), coconut or rice spirit

araignée *nf* (of meat) ox hock bone meat; (of fish) **~ de mer** spider crab

arbois *nm* Franche-Comté wine

arbolade *nf* cream custard; sweet omelette

arbouse *nf* arbutus-berry; strawberry-tree berry

arc-en-ciel *nm* (of trout) rainbow; grenadine/aniseed/mint/chartreuse cocktail

archiduc *a* archduke; onion/paprika-sauced

ardennaise (à l') *a* of the Ardennes; juniper-sauced

arête *nf* (of fish) bone

argent *nm* silver, cash, money

argenterie *nf* silverware, cutlery

argenteuil *a* asparagus-garnished; asparagus-sauced

argentine (petite) *nf* Mediterranean sea fish: argentine

argile *nf* clay

ariégoise (à l') *a* stuffed-cabbage/potato-garnished

arlésienne (à l') *a* of Arles, eggplant/onion/tomato-garnished

armagnac *nm* Armagnac

armenonville *a* Armenonville, sliced-potato/creamed-morel mushroom-garnished

armoire *nf* cupboard, **~ frigorifique** coldroom, coldstore

armoise *nf* wormwood

armoricain *a* Armorican, of Brittany; (of lobster, now considered:) à l'américaine, garlic/tomato/oil crustacean-sauced

arnoglosse *nm* sea flat fish: arnoglossus, scaldfish

aromate *nm* herb, spice, seasoning

aromatique *a* aromatic

arôme *nm* aroma, (of wine) nose; **~s** piquant Lyon cheeses

arquebuse *nf* Arquebuse, herb

liqueur

arradoy *nm* ewe's milk cheese

arrangement *nm* (of flowers) arrangement

arrhes *nfpl* deposit

arrière-cuisine *nf* scullery

arrière-goût *nm* aftertaste

arrosé *a* sprinkled

arroser *vt* to baste

artagnan (à la d') *a* of d'Artagnan; cep/béarnaise-garnished

artésien *a* (of well) artesian

artichaut *nm* artichoke

Artois (d') *a* (of puff pastry) baked cream/fruit-filled; (of lamb) Madeira sauce/peas/potato croustade-garnished; **potage ~** chervil-flavoured bean soup

asafoetida *nf* asafoetida, condiment gum resin

asapo *nf* chicken-stew soup

ascenseur *nm* lift, elevator

asiago *nm* cow's milk cheese

aspartam(e) *nm* aspartame, sugar substitute

aspe *nm* freshwater fish: asp

asperge *nf* asparagus

aspic *nm* aspic

assaisonner *vt* (of salad) to dress, to flavour

assemblage *nm* (of wine) blending

asseoir (s') *vpr* to sit down

assiette *nf* plate, dish; **~ creuse** soup plate; **petite ~ plate** side plate; **~ plate** dinner plate; **~ anglaise** *(also ~ garnie)* variety of cold meats; **~ composée** cold meat/vegetables

assiettée *nf* dish; plateful

assoiffant *a* thirst-making

assujettir *vt* (of fowl) to tie with string

Asti Spumante *nm* Italian sparkling wine

athénienne (à l') *a* athenian; olive oil/onion-cooked

athérine *nm* small sea fish: sand smelt

atoca *nm* cranberry

attacher *vt* (of milk) to burn

attelet *nf* ornamental skewer

attendrir *vt* to tenderise; to pound

attereau *nm* fried-breadcrumbed-skewered hors d'oeuvres; membrane-wrapped chopped pork/liver

attiédir *vt* to warm-up

attriau *nf* pork-liver/veal/onion/herb sausage

aubépine *nf* hawthorn, may

auberge *nf* tavern, inn

aubergine *nf* aubergine, eggplant

aubrac *nm* Aubrac beef variety

aumônière *nf* purse, pocket; (of fruit) **à l'~** in purse-shaped pancake

auriculaire oreille-de-judas *nm* jew's ear fungus

aurore *nf* dawn; tomato-puréed velouté sauce

autocuiseur *nm* pressure cooker

automne *nm* autumn

autrichienne (à l') *a* austrian-style; paprika-flavoured

autruche *nf* ostrich

auvergnate (à l') *a* of the Auvergne

auxey-duresses *nm* Beaune wine

auxide *nm* sea fish: frigate mackerel

avaler *vt* to swallow, to drink

avancé *a* too ripe, off

aveline *nf* filbert nut; cultivated hazelnut

avgolemono *nf* egg-yolk/lemon soup or sauce

aviculture *nf* poultry-farming

avocat *nm* avocado pear

avoine *nf* oat

avoirdupois *nm* avoirdupois, weight system

axoi *nm* Basque diced veal or duck with peppers

ayu *nm* (of fish) sweetfish

azarole *nf* azarole, hawthorn-like hip

B

baba *nm* baba; rum-soaked cake; **baba ghannouj** eggplant purée

babaco *nf* babaco fruit, papaya-like fruit

babeurre *nm* buttermilk

bac *nm* (of vegetables) rack; vat

bacalau *nm* cod

bacardi *nm* bacardi; rum/grenadine/lemon cocktail

bachique *a* Bacchanalian, of the god of wine

bacon *nm* bacon

badèche *nf* sea fish: sea-perch

badiane *nf* star anise

baeckeoffa *nm* slow-cooked meat stew

bagages *nmpl* luggage

bagel *nm* bagel, hard ring-shaped bread roll

bagnes *nm* cow's milk cheese

Bagration *a* (of) Princess Bagration

baguette *nf* stick of bread; **~ de Laon** cow's milk cheese

baie *nf* berry; **~s cosmestibles** soft fruit

Bailey's *nf* cream/coffee/whiskey liqueur

bain-marie *nm* double boiling-pan

baiser *nm* small meringue cream cake

baklava *nm* nut/honey pastry lozenge

balai *nm* sea fish: dab, long rough

balance *nf* scales

baleine *nf* whale

baleineau *nm* whale calf

baliste *nm* sea fish: trigger fish

balle *nf* husk

ballon *nm* brandy balloon; wine glass

ballotin *nm* punnet

ballotine *nf* small boned/stuffed

bird or leg of bird with Madeira; fish/meat in aspic

balsamique *a* balsamic

balthazar *nm* balthazar, large champagne bottle (16 ordinary bottles)

bamboche (en) *a* (of cod) fried and with fried-eggs

bambou *nm* bamboo

banane *nf* banana; **~ plantain** plantain

bandol *nm* Provence wine

bandon *nm* flask bung

banette *nf* (of bread) pointed-ended french stick

bannette *nf* pulse

banon *nm* soft goat cheese

banquet *nm* banquet

banqueter *vi* to feast

banquière *a* banquière, chicken/mushroom/truffle-garnished or sauced

banyuls *nm* Roussillon wine

bar *nm* bar; (of fish) sea bass; **~ tacheté** striped bass

barack pálinka *nf* apricot brandy

baratte *nf* butter churn

barbadine *nm* giant granadilla (like passion fruit)

barbarie *nf* Barbary coast; **figue de ~** prickly pear; **canard de ~** muscovy duck

barbe à papa *nf* candyfloss

barbeau *nm* barbel

barbecue *nm* barbecue

barbet *nm* mullet (*see* rouget)

barbillon *nm* small barbel

barbouille (en) *nf* (of ground game) thickened with blood

barbue *nf* brill

bardane *nf* burdock

bardatte *nm* bacon-wrapped hare/rabbit-stuffed cabbage

barder *vt* to bard, to lard

barigoule (à la) *a* stuffed with ham/mushrooms; with braised chopped artichoke; **~** milk-cap mushroom

baril *nm* small cask

barman *nm* bartender, barman

barolo *nm* Italian red wine

baron *nm* (of beef) baron, double sirloin; saddle of lamb

barquette *nf* small oval pastry case

barracuda *nm* barracuda

barre *nf* (of chocolate) bar

barrique *nf* barrel, hogshead

Barsac *nm* sweet Bordeaux wine

bas *nm* **~ de carré** (of veal) middle neck; **~ morceau** (of beef/veal) flank/breast; **~- ventre** underbelly

base (de) *nf* (of diet) staple

baselle *nm* basella, Ceylon spinach

basilic *nm* basil

basquaise (à la) *a* basquaise; Bayonne ham/mushroom/potato-garnished

basses-côtes *nfpl* chuck, blade

bassine à confiture *nf* preserving pan

bastella *nf* meat/vegetable turnover

ba-ta-clan *nm* almond cake

bâtard *nm* Vienna roll

bâtarde *a* (of sauce) bâtarde, mock hollandaise

bâtelière (à la) *a* bâtelière; mushroom/onion/prawn/egg-garnished; with green sauce

bâton de Jacob *nm* Jacob's baton, thin éclair

bâtonnet *nm* (of fish/vegetable) finger

batte *nf* swiss chard

batterie de cuisine *nf* cooking utensils

batteur *nm* (of eggs) beater, mixer

battre *vt* to whip, to whisk, to pound; **~ en neige** (of eggwhite) to whip

baudroie *nf* sea fish: angler fish

baudruche *nf* membrane of large intestine

baumkuchen *nm* layered cardamom spiced spit-made cake

bavarois *a* Bavarian; bavarois, flavoured rich custard

bavette *nf* undercut; skirt; baby's feeder

baveux (euse) *a* runny

bavoir *nm* bib

bayonnaise (à la) *a* Bayonnaise, Bayonne ham-garnished

béarnaise *nf* béarnaise, rich butter sauce

béatilles *nfpl* creamed pastry fillings

béatrix *a* spring vegetable-garnished; (of salad) chicken/potato/asparagus

beaucaire *a* of Beaucaire; celery-including

beauclaire *nm* sea fish: priacanthidae: atlantic bigeye

beaufort *nm* cow's milk cheese

beauharnais *a* Beauharnais, mushroom/artichoke-garnished; (of dessert) banana/rum

beaujolais *nm* beaujolais wine

beauvilliers *a* braised salsify/tomato/spinach/offal-garnished; almond gâteau

bec *nm* (of teapot &c) spout

bécasse *nf* woodcock

bécasseau *nm* young woodcock

bécassine *nf* snipe

béchamel *nf* bechamel sauce, flavoured butter/flour/milk sauce

bêche-de-mer *nm* sea cucumber

bécune *nf* sea fish: syphraena viridensis: barracuda variety

beigne *nm* doughnut

beignet *nm* fritter, doughnut, cruller, cracker

bel paese *nm* soft cow's milk cheese

belle-hélène *a* belle-hélène; (of meat) of various rich garnishes; (of dessert) poached fruit/ice cream/hot chocolate

bellet *nm* Var wine

bellevue (en) *a* cold aspic-glazed

belon *nm* Belon oyster

béluga (bélouga) *nm* sturgeon

variety

bénédicité *nm* grace (before meal)

bénédict *a* (of eggs) benedict; (of poached egg) hollandaise'd on ham and muffin

Bénédictine *nf* Benedictine, liqueur; **à la ~** salt cod-inclusive

bercy *a* (of fish/meat) Bercy, wine/shallot-sauced; (of eggs) scrambled with sausage/tomato sauce garnish

bergamote *nf* bergamot, orange essence; variety of pear

bergerac *nm* Dordogne wine

bergonnette *nf* ewe's milk cheese

berlingot *nm* humbug

bernique *nf* limpet, mollusc

berny *nf* berny, almond-coated croquette potato; lentil purée tartlet

berrichonne (à la) *a* from Berry; (of meat) cabbage/onion/bacon/chestnut-garnished

bérudge *nf* small red plum

béryx *nm* sea fish: beryx

besace du berger *nf* goat cheese

bestiaux *nmpl* cattle

bêtise *nf* mint sweet

bette *nf* swiss chard

betterave *nf* beet, beetroot; **~ à sucre** sugar beet

between-the-sheets *nm* brandy/cointreau/rum/orange cocktail

beuchelle *a* sweetbread/kidney pie creamed mushroom-garnished

beurre *nm* butter; (of meat) tender; **~ blanc** white butter sauce, vinegar/shallot/butter sauce; **~ noir** butter with reduced vinegar; **~ clarifié** ghee or buffalo milk, clarified butter; **~ composé** flavoured butter; **~ de gascogne** Gascony butter, garlic-ed veal fat; **~ de jurançon** with Jurançon wine; **~ manié** manié, butter pasted with flour

beurrier *nm* butter dish

bhaji *nm* spicy indian vegetable fritter

biarrote (à la) *a* cep-garnished

bib gourmand *nm* Michelin® Guide restaurant category (good-value low-cost)

biberon *nm* feeding bottle

bicarbonate *nm* (of soda) bicarbonate

biche *nf* female deer

biche-faon *nf* doe

bichof *nm* (hot) mulled wine; (cold) fruit cup

bidon *nm* milk churn

biens *nmpl* goods

bienvenu *a* welcome!

bière *nf* beer; **~ brune** porter; **~ épicée** wassail

bierschinkenwurst *nf* pork/ham/beef garlic sausage

bierwurst *nf* pork and beef garlic sausage

biftek *nm* beefsteak, steak

bigarade *nf* bitter orange; (of

sauce) bigarade

bigarreau *nm* bigarreau cherry

bigorneau *nm* winkle, periwinkle

bigos *nm* sauerkraut/meat stew

bigouden *a* from Bigouden

bille *nf* (of melon &c) ball

billy by *a* a mussel soup parmesan-garnished

biologique *a* organic, chemical-free

bireweck *nm* kirsch/fruit cake

biriani *nm* (of lamb, chicken or fish) spicy rice stew

biscôme *nm* gingerbread

biscotin *nm* small biscuit for ice cream

biscotte *nf* rusk, melba toast

biscuit *nm* biscuit; ~ **de savoie** sponge cake; ~ **salé** cracker for cheese

bishop *nm* punch

bison *nm* bison

bisque *nf* bisque, rich fish/meat soup

bist(r)ouille *nf* coffee-brandy mix; cheap brandy

bistro(t) *nm* café, bar

blaff *nm* sauced fish or shell-fish

blagny *nm* Beaune red wine

blanc (che) *a* white; **à ~** (in the cooking) uncoloured; **au ~** in stock; **boudin ~** white pudding; **~-cassis** wine/ blackcurrant liqueur aperitif; ~ **de cuisson** juice for cooking white offal/vegetables; ~ **de ~** white wine from white grapes; ~ **fumé** white wine grape

variety; ~ **d'oeuf** albumen, egg-white; ~ **de ~** exclusively-white grape white wine; ~ **de noirs** black grape white wine; some champagnes; **~-manger** blancmange; *nm* white wine; (of poultry) breast

blanchaille *nf* whitebait

blanche *a* (of sauce) blanche, bechamel, white, buttery roux

blanchir *vt* to blanch

blanquette *nf* (of veal) blanquette, fricassée in creamy sauce; ~ **de Limoux** sparkling white wine

blayais *nm* Côtes-de-Blaye wine

blé *nm* corn, wheat; ~ **dur** durum wheat; ~ **noir** buckwheat; ~ **d'inde** maize

blennie *nf* river fish: blenny; sea fish: catfish

blet (tte) *a* over-ripe

blette (bette) *nf* chard, Swiss chard, variety of spinach beet

bleu *a* blue; (of meat) rare, underdone; (of trout) poached; (of cheese) blue; ~ **d'auvergne, ~ de bresse, [and others]** blue cheese

bleuet *nm* cornflower; blueberry

blini *nm* blini, thick pancake (in Russia with caviar and sour cream)

blonde *nf* (of beer) lager, light ale, pils; ~ **d'Aquitaine** beef variety

blondir *vt* to brown

bloody Mary *nm* bloody Mary,

vodka and tomato juice

blue lagoon *nm* curaçao/vodka/ lemon cocktail

bluet *nm* blueberry; blewit mushroom

bocal *nm* fishbowl; wide-mouthed bottle

bock *nm* beer glass

boeuf *nm* beef, ox; **~ à braiser** stewing steak

bogue *nf* (of chestnut) husk, shuck; (of fish) bogue, sea bream

bohémienne (à la) *a* bohémienne; with ratatouille-like garnish

boire *vt* to drink

bois *nm* wood; **fraise de ~** wild strawberry

boisson *nf* drink, beverage; **~ gazeuse** mixer

boîte *nf* (of beer) can; (of bread) bin; (of biscuits) barrel

bol *nm* (of punch) bowl

bolée *nf* bowlful

bolet *nm* boletus mushroom

bollito misto *nm* meat stew

bolognaise (à la) *a* (of pasta) meat and tomato sauced

bombe *nf* mould for ice cream

bon marché *a* cheap, good value

bonbon *nm* sweet, confection; **~ acidulé** acid drop; **~ anglais** fruit-drop; **gros ~ à la menthe** bull's-eye

bonbonne *nf* demijohn

bondard (bondart) (bonde) *nm* cow's milk cheeses

bonde *nf* flask bung

bondon de neufchâtel *nm* cow's milk cheese

bonite *nf* bonito, tuna

bonitou *nm* sea fish: auxis rochei: frigate mackerel

bonne femme *a* (of meat) casserole-cooked

bonne *nf* maid

bonnes-mares *nm* burgundy wine

bonnet *nm* cow's or sheep's stomach; **~ d'évêque** pope's nose, parson's nose

bonnezeaux *nm* Anjou sweet white wine

bontemps *a* (of sauce) cider/ mustard

bord *nm* edge

bordeaux *nm* Bordeaux wine; claret

bordelais (aise) *a* from Bordeaux; (of sauce) red/white wine

bordure *nf* border-of-plate garnish

botte *nf* (of asparagus &c) bunch

bottereau *nm* liqueur fritter

botvinya *nf* spinach/sorrel/ beetroot-leaf soup

bouc *nm* male goat; shrimp

boucan *nm* charcoaled stuffed sheep

boucané *a* smoked

bouche *nf* mouth

bouchée *nf* mouthful; puff pastry-case

boucher *vt* (of bottle) to cork

bouchère (à la) *a* bone marrow-garnished

bouchon *nm* cork; small traditional Lyon restaurant

bouchot *nm* mussel bed

bouclée *a* (of ray) thornback

boudin *nm* pudding; **~ noir** black pudding; **~ blanc** white pudding

boudoir *nm* sponge finger

bougeoir *nm* candlestick

bougie *nf* candle

bougon *nm* soft goat cheese

bougras *nf* vegetable soup

bouillabaisse *nf* bouillabaisse, fish soup

bouillant *a* boiling

bouilleture *nm* eel stew

bouilleur de cru *nm* private distiller

bouilli *nf* boiled; *nm* (of beef) stew

bouillie *nf* porridge, baby's cereal, pulp, mush, flummery; sherried oatmeal jelly with cream

bouillir *vi* to boil

bouilloire *nf* kettle

bouillon *nm* broth, stock, beef tea; bubble; (of soup) clear; (of restaurants) cheap/fixed-price; **~ cube** stock cube; **~ gras** meat stock

boukha *nf* fig liqueur

boulangère (à la) *a* baker's wife-method; oven-cooked, stewed

boule *nf* (of confectionery) **~ de**

gomme fruitgum; (of meal) **~ de bâle** pork sausage; (of dessert) **~-de-neige** cream-covered cake; **~ d'or** french Edam cheese

boulette *nf* meatball, dumpling; **~s de poisson** gefilte (stuffed) fish; **~ d'avesnes**, **~ de cambrai** cow's milk cheese

boulot *nm* whelk

bouquet garni *nm* bouquet garni, bag of herbs for stewing

bouquet *nm* (of fish) prawn; (of wine) nose; (of flowers) bunch

bouquetière (à la) *a* decorative vegetable-garnished

bouquetin *nm* wild goat

bourbon *nm* bourbon whisky

bourdaloue *nf* almond-creamed macarooned pears; fruit with rice/semolina

bourdelot *nf* pastry-covered baked apple

bourgeais *nm* bordeaux wine

bourgeoise (à la) *a* bourgeoise, (usu of meat) family-style

bourgeon *nm* bud, tip

bourgogne *nm* (of wine) burgundy

bourgueil *nm* Touraine wine

bourguignonne (à la) *a* (usu of beef) of Burgundy; stewed in red wine/mushrooms/onions

bourrache *nf* borage, cucumber-flavoured herb

bourriche *nf* game/fish hamper

bourride *nf* (of fish) stew with aïoli

bourriol *nf* potato/flour/milk pancake

bout *nm* end; **~ filtre** (of cigarettes) filter tip

boutargue (poutargue) *nf* botargo, salted pressed mullet roe

boutefas *nf* pork sausage

bouteille *nf* bottle

boutifar *nm* black pudding

bouton-de-culotte *nm* goat cheese

bouvillon *nm* young bullock

bouzy *nm* red champagne

bovines *nmpl* cattle

boyau *nm* animal intestine

boysenberry *nf* boysenberry, large loganberry

brabançonne (à la) *a* of Brabant; glazed Mornay-sauced vegetables

bragance *a* Braganza; béarnaised croquette potato/tomato-garnished

braise *nf* burning charcoal; embers

braisé *a* braised, pot-roasted

braisière *nf* braising pan

brancas *a* shredded/creamed potato/lettuce-garnished

branche *nf* (of celery, asparagus) stick, spear

brandade *nf* brandade; (of cod) in rich creamy sauce

brandza *nm* ewe's milk cheese

brassage *nm* (of beer) brew

brasserie *nf* brasserie, informal restaurant; brewery

brebis *nf* sheep, ewe; **le pur ~** ewe's milk cheese

bréchet *nm* breastbone; wishbone

brèdes *nm* creole-riced spicy bacon-ed vegetable leaves

bréhan *a* artichoke-heart/bean/cauliflower/hollandaise/potato-garnished

brème *nf* bream

bresaola *nm* raw salted beef

brésolles *nf* casseroled layered meat/forcemeat

bressane (à la) *a* of Bresse poultry

breton (onne) *a* Breton; *nm* decorative biscuit pyramid; **à la ~onne** (of braised mutton) with haricot beans

bretzel *nm* pretzel, high-baked cocktail biscuit

breuvage *nm* beverage, drink

Brézil *nm* (of nuts) Brazil

bricelet *nf* sweet or savoury waffle

brick *nm* fritter

bricquebec *nm* cow's milk cheese

brider *vt* (of fowl) to truss

brie *nm* Brie: soft cream cow's milk cheese

brigade de cuisine *nf* kitchen team

brignoles *nf* plum variety

brillat-savarin *nm* cow's milk cheese

brin *nm* sprig

brindamour *nm* soft ewe's milk

cheese

brioche *nf* brioche, baked dough cottage loaf-shaped

brique *nf* ~ **du Forez** goat cheese; ~ **du Livradois** goat cheese

briquet *nm* lighter

brisé *a* (of pastry) short, shortcrust; (of biscuit) broken

Bristol *a* risotto croquette/flageolet/potato-garnished

broc *nm* jug

broccio (brocciu) (brucciu) *nm* ewe's milk cheese

broche *nm* spit

brochet *nm* pike; ~ **de mer** sea fish: sphyraena sphyraena

brocheton *nm* pickerel, young pike

brochette *nf* skewer, kebab (kabab) (kabob)

brocoli *nm* broccoli, calabrais (calabrese)

brodetto *nf* fish soup

bronx *nm* gin/orange/vermouth cocktail

brosme *nm* sea fish: torsk

brou de noix *nf* walnut-husk liqueur

brouet *nm* gruel

broufado *nm* beef/capers/anchovy casserole

brouillés *a* (of eggs) scrambled

brouilly *nm* beaujolais wine

broulaï *nm* fish/potato stew

brousse *nf* ewe's milk cheese

broutart (broutard) *nm* grass-fed calf

brouter *vt* to graze, to nibble, to browse

broye (broyé) *nm* cornmeal broth

broyer *vt* to crush

brugnon *nm* nectarine

brûlé *a* burnt, singed, roasted

brûleur *nm* cooker

brûlot *nm* flamed alcohol

brûlure *nf* scalding

brun *a* (of rice) brown; (of beer) stout

brunch *nm* brunch

brunoise *nf* buttered vegetables/mirepoix garnish

bruschetta *nm* olive-oil toast

brut *a* (of flour) wholemeal; (of champagne) extra dry; (of sugar) unrefined; ~ **sauvage** (of champagne) bone dry

bruxelloise (à la) *a* stewed potato/sprouts/endive-garnished

bruyère *nf* (of honey) heather; (of game) **coq de** ~ capercaillie, large grouse; **petit coq de** ~ black grouse, blackcock

buccin *nm* whelk

bûche de noël *nf* yule log

buffet *nm* sideboard, dresser; buffet, fork lunch, fork supper

buffle (esse) *nm/f* buffalo

buglosse *nf* borage variety

bugne *nf* fried sugared dough strip

buisson *nm* (of presentation) (in a) bush, (in a) pyramid

bulot *nm* whelk

burette *nf* cruet

burlat *nf* cherry variety

buvable *a* drinkable

buvette *nf* café, bar, refreshment stall

buveur (euse) *nm/f* drinker

buzet *nm* south-west France wine

byzantine (à la) *a* braised potato/mushroom/lettuce/creamed-cauliflower side-dished

C

cabardès *nm* Aude wine

cabaret *nm* cabaret

cabassol *nf* white wine-stewed sheep's head

cabécou *nm* soft goat cheese

cabernet franc *nm* Loire/Bordeaux grape variety

cabernet sauvignon *nm* grape variety

caberon *nm* flan

cabessal (en) *a* made round for cooking

cabillaud *nm* cod

cabinet *nm* water closet, WC, toilet

cabochon *nm* (of decanter) stopper

caboulot *nm* small out-of-town café

cabrales *nm* blue cheese

cabus *nm* (of cabbage) white

cacahouette (cacah(o)uète) *nf* peanut, monkey nut, ground nut

cacao *nm* cocoa

cachalot *nm* sperm-whale

cachat *nm* ewe or goat cheese

caciocavallo *nm* cow's milk cheese

cadillac *nm* Bordeaux sweet white wine

cadre *nm* surroundings

café *nm* coffee, café; **~ au lait, (crème)** (of coffee) white; **~ complet** continental breakfast; **~ express** espresso coffee; **~ filtre** filter coffee; **~ instantané (en poudre)** instant coffee; **~ noir (nature)** black coffee; **~ vert** unroasted coffee; **~ liégois** (of ice-cream) coffee

caféine *nf* caffeine

cafétéria *nf* cafeteria

cafetière *nf* coffee-pot, percolator

cageot *nm* (of fruit/fish) crate, case

caghuse (caqhuse) *nf* pork-knuckle/onion stew

cahors *nm* Cahors red wine

caïeu (cayeu) *nm* (of garlic) clove

caille *nf* quail

caillé *a* (of milk) curd, junket

caillebotte *nf* cow or goat cheese; curdled-cream/cream/sugar dish

cailler *vt* to curdle, to congeal

caillette *nf* young quail; flat pork/vegetable sausage

caïon (cayon) *nm* pork

caisse *nf* (of bottles/vegetables) crate, box; cash till, cash point; pastry-case

cajou *nm* (of nuts) cashew

cake *nm* fruitcake, plum-cake

calamar *nm* squid

caldeirada *nf* white-wine fish soup

calebasse *nf* calabash

calibrer *vt* (of eggs &c) to grade by size

calicagère *nf* sea fish: bream variety

calisson *nm* almond/crystallised-fruit sweetmeat

calmar (calamar) *nm* squid

calorie *nf* calorie

caluyau *nm* sea fish: twaite shad (male)

calvados *nm* apple brandy

cambridge *nf* (of sauce) anchovy/mustard/egg-yolk sauce

camembert *nm* soft cream cow's milk cheese

camomille *nf* camomile (chamomile)

campagne (de) *nf* country, farmhouse

canapé *nm* canapé, open sandwich, savoury, small pastry/toast/biscuit base for cocktail nibbles; **~-salle** canapé served at table

canard *nm* duck; **~ laqué** Peking duck

canardeau *nm* duckling

canari *a* melon type

cancalaise (à la) *a* Cancalaise; oyster-garnished

cancoillotte *nf* warm buttered cheese in white wine

candi *a* (of sugar) purified and crystallised

cane *nf* female duck

canestrato *nm* ewe's milk cheese

caneton *nm* duckling

canette *nf* duckling; (of beer) small bottle

canne *nf* (of sugar) cane

canneberge *nf* cranberry

cannelé *nm* small vanilla cake

canneler *vt* (of ornament) to scallop

cannelle *nf* cinnamon

cannelloni *nm* cannelloni, pasta in tube form

canole *nm* dry biscuit

canon *nm* (of wine) measure, glass; (of spirits) shot, slug; cut of meat

canotière (à la) *a* (of freshwater fish) with bâtarde sauce

cantal *nm* cow's milk cheese

cantaloup *nm* cantaloup melon

canthare *nf* sea fish: black bream

cantine *nf* canteen

cantonais *a* Cantonese; rice garnished

capelan (capalin) *nm* small sea fish: poor-cod

capillaire *nf* fern variety

capilotade *nm* left-overs stew;

en ~ (of fruit) pulped

capitaine *nm* sea bass; emperor fish

capiteux (euse) *a* (of wine &c) heady

caponata *nf* celery/tomato/ eggplant/capers cold hors d'oeuvre

cappuccino *nm* cappuccino, coffee topped with white foamed milk chocolate-topped

câpre *nf* caper

capucin *nm* gruyère choux pastry savoury

capucine *nf* nasturtium

caquelon *nm* earthenware simmering pot

carafe *nf* decanter, carafe

carafon *nm* small decanter, small carafe

carambole *nf* carambola fruit, star-fruit

caramel *nm* caramel, burnt-sugar flavouring, fudge; **~ au beurre** toffee; **~ dur** butterscotch

caramélisé *a* caramelised

carangue *nf* sea fish: scad variety

carapace *nf* shell, carapace

carbonade (carbonnade) *nf* (of meat) charcoal-grilled, thick meat stew with beer/crusted bread

carbonique *a* (of gas) carbon dioxide

carcasse *nf* carcass

cardamome *nf* cardamom spice

cardinal *nm* (of sauce) bright red; lobster-garnish; lobster white-sauce; red-fruit iced dessert

cardine *nf* flat sea fish: megrim

cardon *nm* cardoon, sea-kale-like beet

Carême *nm* Marie-Antoine Carême, France's most illustrious cook

cari *nm* curry

caribou *nm* caribou

caricole *nf* winkle

carignan *nm* south-west France red grape variety; **à la ~** *a* foie gras/egg/asparagus-garnished;

carmélite (à la) *a* (of cold chicken) crayfish mousseline/ truffle-garnished

carmen *a* tomato- or pimento-containing

carmenère *nm* pre-phylloxera French grape variety now the national wine of Chile

carmin *nm* carmine, cochineal, bluish-red colouring

Caroline *nf* (of rice) Carolina, medium thick grain (for puddings); small éclair vol-au-vent; (of soup) maize/onion/ paprika

carotte *nf* carrot

caroube *nf* carob, seed pod of carob tree

carpaccio *nm* carpaccio, dressed thin raw beef/fish

carpe *nf* carp

carpeau *nm* young carp

carré nm (of meat) loin, slab; (of chocolate/cake &c) slab, square; **~ de l'Est** soft cow's milk cheese

carrelet nm plaice

carry nm curry; **soupe au ~** mulligatawny

carte nf menu; **à la ~** non-set menu; **~ bancaire** bank card; **~ de crédit** credit card; **~ d'étudiant** student card; **~ des vins** wine-list; **~ de visite** business card

cartilage nm gristle

carton nm carton, punnet

caruchon nm ewe's molk cheese

carvi nm car(r)away

casier nm (of wine bottles) bin, bottle rack

cassate nf cassata, Neapolitan fruit/nut ice-cream

cassé a broken; **pois ~s** split peas, pease pudding; **cuire au ~** to crystallise

casse-croûte nm snack

casse-noisettes nm nutcrackers

casser vt (of nuts) to crack; (of wine) to spoil; (of solid) to snap off, to break

casserole nf casserole, lidded pot, saucepan; food cooked in ~ (lengthily)

casseron nm fried cuttlefish

cassis nm blackcurrant; blackcurrant liqueur

cassolette nf earthenware dish; deep-fried batter case filled with savoury mix

cassonade nf brown sugar, demerara

cassoulet nm cassoulet, haricot-bean/pickled-goose hot-pot

castagnole (grande) nf ray's bream

castiglione (à la) a castiglione, mushroom-garnished

castillane (à la) a (of beef, lamb) castillane, olive oil/tomato purée-garnished

catalane (à la) a Catalan; tomato/chestnut/sausage/olive-garnished

cauchat a (of fish) bechamel-sauced

cauchoise (à la) a (of jugged hare, rabbit) Caux, apple/mustard/cream-garnished

caudéran (à la) a garlic/shallot/white wine-based

cave nf cellar; **mettre en ~** (of wine) to lay down

caviar nm caviar, roe; **~ rouge** (of salmon) roe

cavour a semolina/ravioli croquette-garnished; truffle/puréed chicken liver-garnished

cayenne nm (of pepper) Cayenne

cédrat nm citron, large but sweeter lemon

céleri nm celery

céleri-rave nm celeriac

célestine nf celestine, fried flambée'd chicken; pancake-garnished tapioca/chicken soup

cellier nm larder

cellulose *nf* (of vegetables) fibre

cendre *nf* ash

cendré *nm* cow's milk cheese

cendrier *nm* ashtray

centrolophe noir *nm* sea fish: black-fish

cépage *nm* variety of vine

cèpe *nm* cep mushroom

céphalopode *nm* mollusc

cépole *nf* sea fish: red band-fish

céréales *nflp* cornflakes

cerf *nm* stag, deer

cerfeuil *nm* chervil

cerise *nf* cherry; **tomate-~** *nm* cherry tomato

cerneau *nm* walnut segment

cerner *vt* to score

cernier *nm* sea fish: wreckfish, stone basse

cérons *nm* bordeaux wine

cervelas *nm* saveloy, small cooked spicy smoked sausage

cervelle *nf* brains; **~ de canut** white wine/shallot/cheese/ crème fraiche Lyon elevenses

cervidé *nm* cervid, deer family

cervoise *nf* barley beer

cétacé *nm* cetacean, whale family

céteau *nm* sole

cévenole (à la) *a* chestnut-including

chabichou *nm* goat cheese

chabot *nm* bullhead, sea scorpion, sea devil

chabrot *nm* soup wine (largely) mixture

chai *nm* wine/spirit store; cellar

chair *nf* (of meat, fruit) flesh; **~ à saucisse** sausagemeat

chaise *nf* chair; **~ haute** high-chair; **~ roulante** wheelchair

chalonnaise (à la) *a* Chalon, sauced cockscombs/kidney/ mushroom/truffle-garnished

chambarand *nm* soft cow's milk cheese

chambertin *nm* burgundy; **poulet ~** burgundy/mushroom-cooked

chambord *a* (of stuffed fish) mushroom/truffle/quenelles-garnished

chambre *nf* room

chambrer *vt* (of wine) to bring to room temperature

chameau *nm* camel

chamois *nm* chamois

champagne *nm* champagne, twice-fermented sparkling French white wine

champêtre *a* rural, rustic, country

champignon *nm* mushroom; **~ noir** jew's ear fungus

champigny *nf* apricot patisserie

champvallon *nm* potato/mutton/ onion bake

chandelier *nm* candlestick

chandelle *nf* candle

chantecler *a* (of lobster, langouste) with curried Nantua sauce

chanterelle *nf* chanterelle mushroom

chantilly (à la) *a* Chantilly, with

flavoured beaten/whipped cream

chaource *nm* cow's milk cheese

chapati *nf* chapati, bread pancake

chapelure *nf* dried breadcrumbs

chapon *nm* capon; garlic crust added to salads; scorpion fish

charbon de bois *nm* charcoal

charbonnier *nm* charcoal-burner

charcuterie *nf* cold cooked pork meats

charcutière (à la) *a* (of charcuterie) gherkin/onion/ white wine-sauced

chardonnay *nm* white grape variety

charentais *a* melon variety

chariot à desserte *nm* trolley

charlotte *nf* charlotte; (of fruit) baked in bread-lined mould

charmoula *nf* charmoula, sweet-and-sour sauce

charnu *a* (of wine) with body; (of fruit) fleshy

charolais *nm* Charolais; (of a breed of cattle) beef; goat cheese

charolaise *nf* (of beef) elbow

charon *nm* sharon-fruit (charon-fruit)

charpenté *a* (of wine) strong in body and alcohol

chartres (à la) *a* Chartres, tarragon-flavoured

chartreuse *nf* Chartreuse, brandy liqueur; mould of choice ingredients

chasselas (fendant) *nm* white wine grape variety

chasseur *a* chasseur; (of sautéed meat) tomato/ mushroom/shallot/white-wine sauce garnished; *nm* pork-beef sausage

châtaigne *nf* chestnut; **~ d'eau** water chestnut

château *nm* castle, palace, mansion; (of potato) sautéed in butter; (of wine) estate

chateaubriand (t) *nm* (of steak) porterhouse, American T-bone; thick-cut slice from heart of fillet of beef (enough for two)

châtelaine (à la) *a* (for simple dishes) rich chestnut- or artichoke-garnished

chatouillard *nm* (of potato) potato strip fried

chauchat *a* (of fish) egg yolk/ butter/béchamel-sauced

chaud *a* hot; (of wine) mulled

chaud-froid *nm* chaudfroid; cold milk or stock flour/aspic sauce

chaudin *nm* pig's intestine

chaudrée *nf* fish soup

chauffe-plat *nm* hot-plate

chauffer *vt* to heat

chausson *nm* turnover, semi-circular covered pastry

chayote *nf* climbing marrow

cheddar *nm* cheddar, hard cow's milk cheese

cheesecake *nm* cheesecake

chef *nm* chef

cheilly-les-maranges *nm*

burgundy wine

cheminée *nf* vent

chemise (en) *a* (in) bladder, wrapped

chemiser *vt* (of receptacle) to line

chénas *nm* beaujolais wine

chêne *nm* oak

chenin blanc *nm* Loire white grape variety

chénopode *nm* goosefoot

chèque *nm* cheque (check); ~ **barré** crossed cheque

cher (chère) *a* expensive

chère *nf* (of food) fare

cherry-blossom *nm* cherry-brandy/brandy/curaçao/grenadine/lemon cocktail

cherry-brandy *nm* cherry brandy

chervis *nm* chervis vegetable

chester *nm* cheddar/cheshire cow's milk cheese

chevaine *nm* chub

cheval *nm* horse; **à ~** (of beef) fried egg-topped

chevaler *vi* presentationally to overlap

chevalière (à la) *a* (of sole) crayfish/mushroom/oyster/truffle/tomato sauce-garnished; (of eggs) kidney/mushroom/cockscomb/velouté-garnished

cheverny *nm* Loire wine

chevesne *nm* chub

cheveux d'ange *nmpl* fine vermicelli

chèvre *nf* goat; *nm* goat cheese

chevreau (ette) *nm* kid, young

goat

chevret *nm* goat cheese

chèvreton *nm* goat cheese

chevrette *nf* kid, young nannygoat; roe; prawn

chevreuil *nm* roe deer; venison

chevrotin des aravis *nm* goat cheese

chiboust *a* (of cream) Chiboust, pastry cream

chicha *nf* chicha, maize liquor

chiche *a* meagre; **pois ~** chickpea; **~-kebab** shish kebab

chicon *nm* cos lettuce, endive

chicorée *nf* endive; (of coffee) chicory

chien de mer *nm* dog-fish, huss, small shark

chiffonade *nf* chiffonade, shredded green vegetables

chiffre *nm* digit, number

chil(l)i con carne *nm* chili-spiced beef stew

chimay *nf* beer; **à la ~** (of chicken) noodles/mince-stuffed; (of egg) au gratin with mushrooms

chinchard *nm* scad, horse mackerel

chinois *a* Chinese; strainer; ~ **confit** crystallised small bitter orange

chinon *nm* Loire wine

chinonaise (à la) *a* sausage-stuffed cabbage/potato-garnished

chipirons *nmpl* squid

chipolata *nf* chipolata; **à la**

~ chestnut/onion/carrot/mushroom/bacon/chipolata-garnished

chips *nmpl* crisps

chique *nf* mint-flavoured almond-filled sugar confection

chiqueter *vt* to adorn pastry edge

chiroubles *nm* beaujolais wine

chivry *nm* flavoured herb butter

chlorophylle *nf* chlorophyll

chocolat *nm* chocolate; ~ **au lait** milk chocolate; ~ **à croquer** dark chocolate; ~ **en poudre** drinking chocolate

choesels *nf* onion/beer meat casserole

choiseul *nf* truffle/sauced sole

choisy *a* lettuce-garnished

choix *nm* choice

chop suey *nm* chop suey, mixed meat/rice/onion

chope *nf* mug

chopine *nf* (of wine) bottle

chorba *nf* lamb/vegetable/fruit soup

chorizo *nm* chorizo, spicy pork sausage

choron *a* (of sauce) Choron, tomato-ed béarnaise

chou *nm* small puff pastry, paste of butter/flour/eggs; ~ **à la crème** cream puff; cabbage; ~ **cru (salade de)** cole-slaw; ~ **de Bruxelles** Brussels sprout; ~ **frisé** kale (kail); ~ **précoce** spring greens

chou-fleur *nm* cauliflower

chou-navet *nm* swede; kohlrabi

chou-rave *nm* kohlrabi

choucroute *nf* sauerkraut, fermented cabbage

chouquette *nf* sugared bun

choux *nm* (of pastry) choux

chouze *nm* Anjou cheese

chrysanthème *nm* chrysanthemum

chutney *nm* chutney; condiment

ciboule *nf* spring onion

ciboulette *nf* chive

cicerelle *nf* sea fish: smooth sand-eel

cidre *nm* cider; ~ **fermier** rough cider, scrumpy

cigale *nf* langouste variety

cigare *nm* cigar

cigarette *nf* cigarette; cylindrical biscuit

cigarillo *nm* cheroot

cinsaut (cinsault) *nm* red (Rhône) grape variety

cinghalaise (à la) *a* Sri Lankan; vinaigrette/curry/vegetable salpicon-garnished

cinq-épices *nm* five chinese spices, star anise/clove/fennel/cinnamon/pepper

cinquième *a* fifth; ~ **gamme** heat preservation treatment; ~ **quartier** offal and unusable parts of animal

cioppino *nm* cioppino, white wine/tomato-stewed seafood

ciorba *nf* fish/chicken soup

cipâte (cipaille) *nf* game pâté in pastry-case; sea pie; fruit tart

circuler *vi* to circulate, to hand round

cire *nf* (of bee) wax

ciseaux (cisailles) *nmpl* scissors

ciselé *a* chopped

cîteaux *nm* cow's milk cheese

citron *nm* lemon; **~ vert** lime; **au ~** (of whisky &c) sour

citronnade *nf* still lemonade

citronné *a* lemon-sprinkled

citronnelle *nf* citronella oil; lemon liqueur

citrouille *nf* pumpkin, squash

citrus *nmpl* citruses

cive *nf* spring onion

civelle *nf* young eel

civet *nm* stew; **~ de lièvre** jugged hare; *a* (of soup) thin

civette *nf* chive

clafoutis *nm* black cherry gateau

clairet *nm* deep-pink bordeaux wine

clairette de die *nf* sparkling Drôme wine; white wine grape variety

clam *nm* clam

clamart *a* Clamart, with peas

claquebitou *nm* goat cheese

clarence *a* Clarence, with curried sauce

clarifier *vt* (of butter &c) to clarify

classer *vt* (of fruit &c) to grade by quality

classique (méthode) *a* (of sparkling wine) champagne method

clat *nm* splinter, piece, fragment

clavaire *nm* clavaria mushroom: fairy club

clémentine *nf* clementine, variety of tangerine

clerment *nf* of Clermont-Ferrand; chestnut- or cabbage-garnished

clientèle *nf* customers, clients, guests

climat *nm* (of wine) vineyard; wine-growing field

climatiseur *nm* air-conditioner

clisse *nf* (of tray/bottle) wicker

clitocybe *nm* clitocybe mushroom

clitopile petite prune *nm* mushroom variety: the miller

cloche *nf* bell; dish cover

cloque *nf* (of fruit trees) blight

clou de girofle *nm* clove

clouter *vt* (of onions) to stick with cloves; (of meat/fish) to stick with *(e.g.)* garlic

clovisse *nf* clam

coaguler *vpr* (of milk) to curdle

cobaye *nm* guinea-pig

cochenille *nf* cochineal

cochon *nm* pig; **~ de lait** sucking-pig; **~ d'Inde** guinea-pig

cochonaille *nf* pork

cocktail *nm* cocktail, mixed alcoholic/non-alcoholic drink; hors d'oeuvre; cocktail party; **~ de crevettes** shrimp cocktail

coco (noix de) *nf* coconut

cocotte *nf* casserole, pot; **oeufs en ~** baked eggs, shirred eggs

code postale *nm* zip code, post

code

coeur nm (of meat/fruit) heart; (of apple) core; ~ **de neufchâtel** cow's milk cheese

coffre nm breast

coffret nm (of cigars) box; (of liqueurs) cabinet

cognac nm cognac, brandy

coiffe nf caul, membrane used to protect meat in cooking

coin-repas nm dining area, dinette

coing nm quince

cointreau nf Cointreau®, orange liqueur

col nm (of bottle) neck

cola nm cola

colbert a (of fish) breadcrumbed

colère (en) a (of fish) fried tail-in-mouth/tomato-sauced

colin nm saithe, coal-fish, coley; ~ **de virginie** partridge

colineau (colinot) nm small barbel

collation nf light meal

colle nf (of fish) glue, isinglass; melted aspic, softened gelatine

coller vt (of wine) to clarify

collet nm (of meat) neck, scrag end, collar

collier nm (of meat) neck, collar

collioure nm Roussillon red/rosé wine

collybie pate-de-velours nf mushroom collybia variety: velvet stem, winter fungus

colombard nm white south-west France grape variety

colombe nf dove

colombine nf breadcrumbed croquette hors d'oeuvre

colombo nf mixed spices

colrave (chou pommé) nm cabbage variety

colvert nm mallard, wild duck

colza nm rapeseed, colza

comestible a edible; ~**s** nmpl fine foods; up-market foods

comète-maquereau nf sea fish: scad variety

cominée nf cumin-ed dish

commander vt to order

commodore a crayfish bisque seafood-garnished

commune nf (of wine) parish

complémentaire a complementary

complémentation nm supplement

complet (ète) a full; (of rice) brown; (of bread) wholemeal

compliment nm compliment

composée a (of salad) mixed; (of sauce) side (sauce)

compote nf compote, stewed fruit

compoter vt to slow-cook

compotier nm raised serving dish

compotier nm large fruit bowl

compris a included; **tout ~** all included

comptoir nm drinks counter

comté nm cow's milk cheese

concasser vt to crush, chop coarsely; (of pepper) to grind;

maïs ~é et bouilli hominy grits
concentré *a* (of milk) condensed; (of meat) extract; concentrated
concombre *nm* cucumber
concorde *a* mashed-potato/baby-carrot/peas-garnished
condé *a* (of savouries) Condé; with kidney-bean purée; (of pastry) almond icing-ed; (of desserts) rice with fruit
condiment *nm* condiment; flavour or piquancy-enhancing additive; chutney; **service à ~(s)** cruet
condition *nf* condition
condrieu *nm* Rhône white wine
confection *nf* (of meals) preparation, concoction
confectionner *vt* (of meals) to prepare
conférence *nf* (of room, pear) conference
confire *vt* to preserve
confiserie *nf* sweetmeat, confectionery
confit *a* crystallised, conserved; (of meat) preserved
confiture *nf* jam, preserve
confort *nm* comfort
congelable *a* freezable
congélateur *nm* deep-freeze
congeler *vt* (of food) to freeze
congolais *nm* coconut-meringue biscuit
congre *nm* conger eel
conservateur *nm* freezer
conserver (se) *vi* to keep, preserve

conserves *nfpl* preserves, tins of, cans of, bottles of
consigne *nf* deposit
consistance *nf* (of liquids) consistency
consommé *nm* consommé, broth, bouillon
consommer *vt* to consume, to eat, to drink
contenance *nf* (of container) capacity
conteneur *nm* container
content *a* happy
conti *a* lentil-garnished
conversation *nf* almond patisserie
convive *nm/f* table-guest
copeau *nm* flake
copieux (euse) *a* (of meal) copious, substantial, solid
coppa *nf* coppa ham
copra *nm* copra, dried coconut kernels
coprin chevelu *nm* mushroom variety: shaggy ink cap (lawyer's wig) (shaggy mane)
coq *nm* cock, chicken; **~ de bruyère** capercaillie, large grouse; **~ nain** bantam; **~ au vin** coq au vin, chicken stewed in wine
coque *nf* cockle; crystallised fruit brioche; (of nuts) hull; **~s à petits fours** fruit-filled almond meringues; (of egg) **à la ~** soft-boiled
coquelet *nm* young cock
coquelicot de Nemours *nm* red-

coloured sugar confectionery

coquetier *nm* eggcup

coquette *nf* sea fish: wrasse

~quillage *nm* shell fish meat

coquille *nf* (of fish/nuts) shell, scallop; nut shell; (of butter) roll; (of food) scallop-presented; **~ Saint-Jacques** scallop

corail *nm* (of lobster) coral, red part

corb (courbine) *nm* sea fish: meagre variety

corba *nf* meat or fish vegetable soup

corbeille *nf* (of bread, fruit) basket

corbières *nm* Aude wine

cordon bleu *a* cordon bleu; of top culinary quality/ability

corégones *nm* freshwater fish: houting

coriandre *nf* coriander

corinthe (de) *a* (of grapes) currants

cornas *nm* Valence red wine

corne d'abondance *nf* cornucopia, horn of plenty

corned-beef *nm* corned beef, bully beef

cornet *nm* cornet; **~ croquant** brandy snap

cornflakes *nfpl* cornflakes

cornichon *nm* gherkin

corniotte *nf* cream-cheese pastry

cornouille (corniole) (corne) *nf* dogwood fruit

corps *nm* (of wine) body

corroyer *vt* to curry

corsé *a* (of wine) full-bodied; (of food) strong, spicy

coryphène *nf* sea fish: 'rat-tail' variety

cosmestible *a* (of mushrooms &c) edible

cosse *nf* (of peas &c) pod, hull, shuck

costières-de-nîmes *nm* Nîmes wine

côt *nm* (of wine) Loire Malbec

côte *nf* hill, slope; (of meat) chop, rib, chump chop; (of celery) stick; **côte(s)-de(du)-[ ]** wine of [ ]; **~s découvertes** (of lamb) neck

côté *nm* side

coteau *nm* hill, slope; **coteaux-de-[ ]** wine of [ ]

côtelette *nf* cutlet, T-bone meat, *pl* lamb chops; **~s premières** best end of neck

côtier *a* (of fish) inshore

cotignac *nm* quince sweetmeat

cotriade *nf* fish soup

cou *nm* neck

couche *nf* layer

coucoulelli *nm* white wine/olive oil cakes

coudenou *nm* pork rind white pudding or sausage

couenne *nf* rind, skin; **~ rissolée** (of pork) crackling

coulant *a* smooth, runny

coulemelle *nm* mushroom variety: parasol

couler *vt* to inject jelly between paté and its pastry case

coulis *nm* coulis, cullis, sauce, soup, purée

coulommiers *nm* cow's milk cheese

coup *nm* drink, draught, shot, slug; cut; **~ de feu** charring

coupage *nm* (of wine) blending

coupe *nf* dish, glass or silver cup, goblet, fruit-bowl; **~ Jacques** fruit-covered; **~-légumes** vegetable slicer; **~-oeufs** egg slicer; **~-pâte** pastry slicer

coupelle *nf* small dish

couper *vt* (of wine) to blend

couperet *nm* butcher's cleaver

couque *nf* currant-ed brioche, gingerbread, icing-ed pastry

courbine (corb) *nm* sea fish: meagre variety

courge *nf* (of vegetable) marrow

courgette *nf* courgette, small vegetable marrow, zucchini

couronne *nf* crown

court-bouillon *nm* court-bouillon, stock for poaching fish/meat

couscous *nm* couscous, farinaceous stew

couscoussier *nm* (of saucepans) steamer

cousinat *nm* chestnut/celeriac/onion soup; vegetable/ham ragout

cousinette *nf* spinach/sorrel/lettuce/vegetables soup

coût *nm* cost

couteau *nm* knife; **~ à découper** carving knife; **~ à pain** bread knife; **~-scie** serrated knife; (of apple) **à ~** dessert apple; razor clam

coûter *vti* to cost

couve *nm* lemon/vanilla cake

couvercle *nm* (of casserole/pan) lid

couvert *nm* place setting; cover charge; *pl* cutlery

cozido *nm* sausage/vegetable/black or white pudding stew

crabe *nm* crab

crachoir *nm* spittoon

cracker *nm* (of biscuits) cracker

crambe *nm* sea-kale

cramique *nm* raisin-ed brioche

crapaud *nm* toad; **~ de mer** angler fish

crapaudine (en) *a* spatchcocked

crapiau (grapiau) *nm* savoury pancake; battered brandied apple

craquant *a* crisp, crunchy

craquelin *nm* brioche with crystallised sugar; (of biscuits) cracker, cracknel, water biscuit

craquelot *nm* smoked young herring

craterelle *nf* mushroom variety: horn of plenty, black trumpet

création *nf* creation

crèche *nf* crèche

crécy (à la) *a* carrot-containing

crémant *nm* sparkling white wine

crème *nf* cream; (of coffee)

white; **~ anglaise** custard; **~ brûlée (caramélisée)** crème brûlée, burnt brown sugar-covered cream custard; **~ de cacao** crème de cacao, chocolate liqueur; **~ caramel** crème caramel, caramelised egg custard; **~ catalane** caramelised lemon/cinnamon pastry cream; **~ chantilly** Chantilly cream, vanilla-ed whipped cream; **chou à la ~** cream puff; **~ de cassis** cassis, blackcurrant liqueur; **~ de menthe** crème de menthe, peppermint liqueur; **~ de tartre** cream of tartar; **~ fraîche** yoghurt-like cheese; **~ fraîche liquide** single-cream; **~ instantanée** custard powder; **~ renversée** custard

crémer vt to add cream

crémet nf Dauphinois milk curd

cremeux (euse) a creamy

crénilabre nm sea fish: wrasse variety

créole a (of rice) creole; pilaff of meat with peppers/tomatoes

crêpe nf pancake; **petite ~ épaisse** crumpet, pikelet, flapjack

crépine nf thin membrane

crépinette nf fag(g)ot; flat sausage

crépy nm Savoie white wine

cresson nm watercress, cress

cressonnière nf bed of watercress

crête de coq nf cockscomb

creusois nm hazel-nut cake

crever (faire) vt (of rice) to de-starch

crevette nf shrimp; **~ rose** prawn

criblé a sifted, graded

crique nf potato/egg pancake

cristal nm crystal

criste-marine nf seaweed variety

cristivomer nm mountain freshwater fish: trout variety, salmonidae

crocodile nm crocodile

croisé a folded

croissant nm croissant, crescent-shaped breakfast pastry

croquant a crunchy, crisp; nm gristle

croquante nf sugar confectionery; small crunchy biscuit; large decorative pâtisserie

croque madame nm toasted cheese/ham/fried egg sandwich

croque monsieur nm toasted cheese/ham sandwich

croque au sel (à la) a with salted raw vegetables, salted crudités

croque-en-bouche nm decorative pyramid of meringue or chou pastry

croquer vt to crunch, to munch; (of chocolate) **à ~** plain chocolate

croquet nm almond finger biscuit

croquette nf croquette, balls of

deep-fried breaded chicken/ potato; **~ de poisson** fish-cake

croquignole *nm* biscuit; icing-covered cake

crosne *nm* Chinese artichoke

crosse *nf* (of beef) leg, knuckle

crotte *nf* (of chocolate) whirl

crottin de chavignol *nm* goat cheese

croupion *nm* (of poultry) parson's nose, pope's nose

croustade *nf* croustade, fried bread savoury case

croustillant *a* crunchy, crusty (also a noun)

croustille *nf* crust

croûte *nf* crust; pastry-case; rind; **~au(x)** (of cooked mushrooms/ cheese &c) on toast

croûton *nm* crouton, crust

crozet *nm* walnut-oil mashed-potato quenelle

cru *a* raw, uncooked; *nm* wine; vintage; vineyard; **grand ~** (of wine) high quality; specific vineyard; **grand ~ classé** (of Médoc & Graves) classed (1855) growth; **premier ~** second (after grand ~) class of Bergundy vineyard

cruchade *nf* cornflour gruel

cruche *nf* earthenware jug

cruchon *nm* small jug

crudités *nmpl* crudités, raw vegetables/fruit

crumble *nm* crumble

crustacé *a/nm* shellfish, lobster, crustacean; **~s** seafood

cube *nm* cube

cuchaule *nf* saffron bread

cueillette *nf* (of fruit) crop

cueillir *vt* to pluck; to pick; to gather

cuiller *nf* scoop, spoon, spoonful; **~ de service** tablespoon

cuillère *nf* spoon

cuillerée *nf* spoonful; **~ à café** teaspoonful; **~ à soupe** ladleful; **grosse ~** heaped spoonful

cuire *vt* to cook, to bake; **trop ~** to overcook; **à ~** (of apples/ chocolate &c) cooking

cuiseur *nm* large cooking pan

cuisine *nf* cuisine, cookery, cooking, kitchen; **élément de ~** kitchen units; **arrière-~** scullery; **~ bourgeoise** simple cooking

cuisiner *vt* to cook

cuisinette *nf* kitchenette

cuisinier (ière) *nm/f* cook; **cuisinière à gaz** gas cooker

cuisse *nf* leg, thigh; (of fruit) **~-madame** kirsch fritter

cuisson *nf* cuisson, baking, cooking, roasting; cooking-time; cooking juices from fish/meat

cuissot (cuisseau) *nm* (of venison/veal) haunch

cuivre *nm* copper

cul-de-poule *nm* handle-less bowl

cul-de-poulin *nm* prime rump

culinaire *a* culinary

culotte *nf* (of beef) rump, aitchbone

cultivateur *nf* salted pork belly/vegetable soup

cumin *nm* cum(m)in; car(r)away; **~ noir** nigella

curaçao *nm* curaçao, gin or brandy-based orange liqueur

curcama *nm* curry ingredient; colourant

curé nantais *nm* cow's milk cheese

cure-dent *nm* toothpick

curiosité *nf* curiosity

curry *nm* curry; **soupe au ~** mulligatawny

cussy (à la) *a* Cussy, with [various] garnishes

cuvage *nm* fermentation

cuve *nf* vat

cuvée *nf* vintage, vatful; (of wine) blend; **~ du patron** house wine

cygne *nm* swan

cyrniki *nm* cottage-cheese dumpling

D

dacquois *a* from Dax; **~e** layered almond meringue

daguet *nm* 2-year old stag

daim *nm* fallow deer

daine *nf* doe

daïquiri *nm* daiquiri, rum/lime-juice cocktail

damas (prune de) *nm* damson

dame-blanche *nf* pale-coloured dessert; meringue-covered cream and crystallised-fruit sponge cake

dame-jeanne *nf* demijohn

damier *nm* praline-covered rum sponge cake

dampfnudeln *nm* cinnamon flavoured fruit patisserie

danablu *nm* cow's milk cheese

danicheff *a* (of salad) of artichoke/mushroom/celeriac/asparagus/potato; (of dessert) praline/coffee/rum ice-cream

dão *nm* Portuguese wine

darblay *nf* vegetable/potato/chervil soup

dariole *nf* dariole, castle pudding mould

darne *nf* (of fish) steak

darphin *nm* potato cake

dartois *nm* Dartois, hot puff-pastry canapé; (of dessert) pastry cream

datte *nf* date

daube *nf* stew

daubière *nf* stewpot

daumont (à la) *a* crayfish/mushroom/Nantua sauce-garnished

dauphin *nm* soft cow's milk cheese

dauphine *a* (of potatoes) mashed/deep-fried; (of vegetable) **à la ~** of deep-fried puréed celeriac/eggplant; (of meat) with dauphine potatoes

dauphinois *a* (of dish) with cream and cheese; **à la ~e** from Dauphiné, of varied garnishes

daurade (dorade) *nf* sea bream, gilt-head bream

débarrasser *vt* (of table) to clear

débit de fritures *nm* fish and chip shop

déborder *vi* to boil over

déboucher *vt* to uncork

décaféiné *a* de-caffeinated

décanter *vt* to decant

décapode *nm* decapod, ten-legged/tentacled crustacean *(incl* lobster, squid)

décapsuleur *nm* bottle-opener

déchet *vt* (of meat) waste

décilitre *nm* decilitre

déclinaison *nf* (of recipe) derivative, deviation, variant

décoction *nf* decoction, essence through boiling

décongeler *vt* (of food) to defrost

décor *nm* decor

décoration *nf* decoration; (of cakes) piping

décortiqué *a* shelled

découper *vt* to carve, to cut, to joint; **couteau à ~** carving-knife

découpoir *nm* pattern-cutting knife

décuire *vt* to slowly add cold water

défait *a* broken, chopped

défarde *nf* lamb's-foot/tripe stew

défendu *ptp of vt* (of smoking, dogs &c) not allowed, forbidden

défourner *vt* to remove from oven

dégeler *vt* to thaw

dégivrer *vt* (of fridge) to defrost

déglacer *vt* to deglaze

dégorger *vt* to drain; to sweat; to remove strong taste of; to soak

dégraissage *nm* the skimming-off of surface fat

dégustation *nf* sampling, savouring

dehors *adv* (of dining) outside; at a restaurant

déjeûner *nm* lunch; **~ d'affaires** business lunch; **~ de travail** working lunch; *vt* to lunch

délice *nm* delight

délicieux (ieuse) *a* delicious

demi *a* half; **~-bouteille** half-bottle; **cuit à ~** half-cooked, parboiled; **~-deuil** (of chicken, turkey) demi-deuil, sliced with interleaved truffles; (of ingredients) black and white; **~-douzaine** half dozen, six; **~-fin** (of peas) small; **~-glace** demi-glace, bone-stock rich brown sauce; **~-pension** half board, dinner bed & breakfast; **~-sec** (of wine) medium; **~-sel** (of butter) slightly salted; soft cow's milk cheese; **~-tarif, ~-place** half price

demi-bec *nm* sea fish: hyporhamphus: picart's halfbleak

demidof *a* (of chicken) Demidof, sautéed

déminéralisé *a* distilled

demoiselle de Cherbourg *nf* small Breton lobster

dénerver *vt* to remove membranes/tendons

dénoyauteur (énoyauteur) *nm* de-stoner

denrée *nf* foodstuff, commodity

dent-de-lion *nf* dandelion

dentelle *nf* (of pancake) thin

denti (denté) *nm* dentex fish; sea bream

dents de scie (à) *nfpl* (of knife) serrated

dents de loup *nfpl* triangular croutons decorative garnish

dépecer *vt* (of meat) to joint

dépôt *nm* (of wine) crust, sediment

dépouiller *vt* to skin, to skim off

derby (à la) *a* (of chicken) Derby, foie gras/rice/truffle-stuffed; (of onion soup) rice/truffle/foie gras-garnished; *nm* cow's milk cheese

dérober *vt* to skin, to peel

derrière *nm* hindquarters

derval *a* artichoke-garnished

dés *nmpl* dice

désaltérer *vt* to quench, to slake

descar *a* chicken-stuffed artichoke heart-garnished

déshydraté *a* dehydrated, dried, instant

désintoxiquer *vt* to detox

désossé *a* boned, filleted

dessalement *nm* desalination

desséché *a* desiccated, stale, dry

dessécher *vt* to desiccate

dessert *nm* dessert, pudding, confection

desserte *nf* left-overs; food made from left-overs; sideboard

desservir *vt* (of table) to clear

dessiccation *nf* desiccation

dessous *adv* under

dessous-de-plat *nm* table mat

dessous-de-verre (-bouteille) *nm* coaster

dessus *adv* above, over

détail *nm* butcher-cut meat

détailler *vt* to dice

détendre *vt* (of cooking) to soften

déthéiné *a* (of tea) decaffeinated

détrempe *nf* flour and water paste

détremper *vt* to soak

devoir *vt* to owe

dévorer *vt* to devour

diable (à la) *a* devilled, spiced with pepper/mustard, hot in taste; *nm* earthenware pot

diablotin *nm* baked grated cheese-covered bread; small measuring spoon

diabolo *nm* diabolo, lemonade/ fruit syrup drink; mint/grenadine drink

diane (à la) *a* (of venison) spicy cream/truffle sauced; game purée; tomato demi-glace stewed

dieppoise (à la) *a* of Dieppe; (of fish) white wine white-sauced

diète *nf* diet

diététique *a* (of restaurant) organic; **aliment ~** healthfood

digérer *vt* to digest

digestif *nm/a* digestive; post-prandial liqueur/spirits

dijonnaise (à la) *a* of Dijon; mustard-flavoured; blackcurrant-including

diluer *vt* to dilute

dinde *nf* turkey

dindon *nm* male turkey

dindonneau *nm* young turkey

dîner *vi* to dine; *nm* dinner, dinner party; ~ **d'affaires** business dinner

dîneur (euse) *nm/f* diner

diot *nf* vegetable-pork sausage

dip *nm* dip

diplomate *nm* trifle; lobster sauce; **à la** ~ *a* lobster/truffle-inclusive

dissoudre (se) *vi* to dissolve, to melt

distance *nf* distance

distiller *vt* to distil(l)

distributeur automatique de billets *nm* cash machine; ticket machine

dodine *nf* duck fillet with mushroom/wine sauce; boned stuffed braised poultry

dolic (dolique) *nm* haricot variety bean

dolma (dolmade) *nm* stuffed vine leaf

domaine *nm* (of wine) estate

dorade (daurade) *nf* sea bream, gilt-head bream

doré *a* adorned with

dorée *nf* sea fish: dory, John Dory

dorer *vt* to brown

doreye *nf* rice tart

doria *a* (of dish) Doria, green/white/red; white-truffled

dormeur *nm* crab

dos *nm* back

dosa *nf* rice pancake

dose *nf* (of alcohol) measure

double *a* double

douceâtre *a* soft, mild, too soft

doucette *nf* corn salad; lamb's lettuce

douceur *nf* sweetness, smoothness

douillon *nm* apple/pear baked in batter

doum *nm* palm wine

doux (douce) *a* (of water) freshwater; (of taste) sweet; not strong; (of wine) pudding wine; (of butter) unsalted; **à feu** ~ on low heat

dragée *nf* sugared almond; comfit; nut-containing sweet

dragéifié *a* sugar-coated

drambuie *nf* Drambuie®, whisky liqueur

dresser *vt* to arrange on plate decoratively; to roll out pastry

droit de bouchon *nm* corkage

dry *nm* vermouth/gin/olive cocktail

du barry *a* cauliflower-containing

dubley *a* mushroom/potato/mushroom purée-garnished

duchesse *nf* duchesse, sweet or savoury filled choux pastry; purée potato with butter/milk/

egg-yolk baked; pear dessert; butter-creamed meringue; **à la ~** *a* with duchesse potato; (of patisseries) almond-containing

dugléré *a* (of fish) Dugléré, poached with parsley/tomato/cream sauce

dur *a* hard; (of egg) hard-boiled; (of cheese) hard; stale; (of meat) tough

durion *nm* durian fruit

duroc *a* Duroc; (of meat) new potato/tomato/chasseur sauce-garnished

duse *a* Duse, potato/tomato/bean-garnished

duxelle *nf* duxelles, mushroom/shallot/herb mince

E

eau *nf* water; **~ de rose** rosewater; **~ de Seltz** soda water; **~ douce** freshwater; **~ de source** spring water; **~ gazeuse** fizzy water; **~ minérale** mineral water; **~ plate** still water; **~ potable** drinking water; **~ rougie** wine and water; **melon d'~** watermelon

eau-de-vie *nf* (of fruit) brandy

ébarber *vt* (of fish) to de-fin

ébullition *nf* (of water) boiling

écaille *nf* (of fish) shell; scale; (of vegetable) layer

écailler *vt* (of shellfish) to open; (of fish) to scale; *nm* seafood merchant

écaler *vt* (of nuts) to shell, to hull

écarlate (à l') *a* of pickled pork/beef/ox tongue

échalote *nf* shallot, scallion

échaudé *nm* (of biscuit) cracker

échézeaux *nm* burgundy wine

échine *nf* loin, chine

éclade (églade) *nf* pine needle-cooked mussels

éclair *nm* éclair, long cream chocolate/moka patisserie

écorce *nf* (of fruit) peel, skin

Ecosse *n* Scotland; **à l'écossaise** (of soup) mutton/barley/vegetable

écosser *vt* (of peas &c) to shell, to hull

écrasé *a* crushed, flattened

écraser *vt* to squash, to crush

écrémé *a* (of milk) skimmed

écrémer *vt* to remove the cream; (of milk) to separate

écrevisse *nf* freshwater crawfish (crayfish)

écrin *nm* case

écuelle *nf* (of bowl) porringer

écume *nf* foam, froth

écumer *vt* to skim

écureuil *nm* squirrel

édam *nm* cow's milk cheese

edelzwicker *nm* Alsace white wine

Edouard VII *a* Edward VII; (of fish) oyster mousseline-sauced; (of chicken) foie gras/rice/truffle-stuffed with red pepper/curry sauce; (of egg) with tongue/truffles

édulcorant *nm* (of tea, coffee) sweetener

effiler *vt* to top-and-tail, to string, to slice in strips

effrité *a* crumbled

eggflip *nm* eggflip (with spirits), eggnog

églantier (fruit d') *nm* hip

églefin *nm* haddock

égoutter *vt* to strain, to drain

égouttoir *nm* strainer, colander, draining-board, dishrack

égrener *vt* (of peas &c) to pod

égrugeoir *nm* mortar

égyptienne (à l') *a* rice/eggplant or tomato-accompanied; (of soup) rice/leek/onion/milk-based

élaborer *vt* (of champagne &c) to elaborate; to develop

élan *nm* elk

élevage (d') *nm* (of fish) farmed

éleveur (euse) *nm/f* breeder; **négociant ~** (of wine) buying-maturing-bottling-selling merchant

emballer *vt* to wrap for cooking

embosser *vt* to mould

embroché *a* spit-roast

émeu (émou) *nm* emu

émietté *a* crumbled

émincé *a* thinly sliced; *nm* thin slice

émissole *nf* seafish: dogfish, small shark, smoothhound

emment(h)al *nm* cow's milk cheese

empanada *nm* pasty

empereur *nm* sea fish: orange roughy

empiler *vt* (of dishes) to stack

emplir *vt* to fill

émulsion *nf* emulsion

émulsionner *vti* to emulsify, to homogenize

en-cas *nm* snack

enchaud *nm* casseroled pork tenderloin

encore *adv* more

encornet *nm* squid

encre *nf* ink

endaubage *nm* braising accompaniments

endive *nf* chicory

enfariné *a* floured

enfourner *vt* to place in oven

engloutir *vt* to devour

engrais *nm* fertilizer

engraissement *nm* (of animals) fattening-up

enivrant *a* (of alcohol) intoxicating, heady

énoyauteur (dénoyauteur) *nm* de-stoner

enrichi *a* supplemented-by

enrober *vt* to coat

entêtant *a* (of alcohol) intoxicating, heady

entier (ère) *a* whole

entonnoir *nm* funnel

entrailles *nfpl* entrails, guts

entrammes *nm* Anjou soft cheese

entrecôte *nf* entrecôte steak, top part of sirloin or ribs of beef

entrée *nf* entrée; first course; *(usu)* main course; formerly a dish after fish course and before the roast

entrelarder *vt* to interlard

entremêler *vt* to interlard

entremet *nm* dessert; side-dish

entresol *nm* mezzanine

épais (se) *a* thick

épaissir *vt* to thicken

épaule *nf* shoulder

épeautre *nm* spelt, wheat

épée *nf* (of fish) swordfish

épépiner *vt* (of fruit) to de-seed

éperlan *nm* sea fish: smelt, sparling

épi de maïs *nm* corn on the cob

épice *nf* spice; **pain d'~** gingerbread

épicurien (ne) *a/nm/f* epicurean

épigramme *nf* epigramme; boned and breaded fried best end of neck or breast of lamb

épinard *nm* spinach

épine *nf* thorn; spine; **~ blanche** hawthorn; **~ noire** blackthorn; **~-vinette** variety of berry; **~ dorsale** backbone

épineux (euse) *a* prickly; (of fish) spiny

épluche-légumes *nm* (of potatoes/carrots &c) peeler

éplucher *vt* (of fruit/vegetables) to clean; to do; to peel; to skin; to unwrap

époisses *nm* soft cow's milk cheese

épurer *vt* to filter

équeuter *vt* (of berries) to shell, to hull; to remove stalk

équilibré *a* (of wine) balanced

équille *nf* sand-eel

équipe *nf* (of kitchen) team; staff

équipement *nm* equipment

érable *nm* maple

ersatz *nm* inferior substitute, ersatz

ésau *a* (of soup) lentil

escabèche *nf* escabèche, marinated fish

escalope *nf* escalope, boneless slice of meat *(usu* veal); **~ viennoise** wiener schnitzel

escalopine *nf* small escalope

escargot *nm* snail; **~ de mer** whelk; **~ aux raisins** pastry cream/raisin-ed brioche

escarole *nf* (of chicory) escarole

escompte *nm* discount

espadon *nm* swordfish

espagne (melon d') *nf* honeydew melon

espagnole *a* (of sauce) espagnole, rich brown mirepoix sauce with tomato/sherry; **à l'~** tomato/rice/peppers/onion/madeira sauce-garnished

espèce *nf* species; **~(s)** money

essence *nf* essence; flavouring

essuy-tout *nm* kitchen roll

essuyer *vt* (of dishes) to dry up, to wipe, to clean, to do

estaminet *nm* bistro, tavern

estival *a* summery

estofinado *nm* estofinado, salt cod provençale

estomac *nm* stomach

estouffade *nf* (of beef) stew; strong clear broth

estragon *nm* tarragon

estuaire (terre et estuaire) *nm* estuary (surf and turf)

esturgeon *nm* sturgeon

établissement *nm* establishment

étain *nm* pewter

étaler (sur) *vt* to spread

étamé *a* (of pans) tinned

étancher *vt* (of thirst) to slake

étape *nf* stopping place

été *nm* summer

étendre *vt* (of pastry) to roll out

éthylotest *nm* breathalyser

étirer *vt* to stretch out

étoile *nf* star

étrille *nf* velvet swimming crab

étriper *vt* to gut, to draw, to clean, to eviscerate

étuvée (étouffée) *nf* jug, braising-pan, steaming-pan

étuver *vt* (of meat) to braise; (of fish) to steam

eucalyptus *nm* eucalyptus

européen *a* european

événement *nm* occasion

éventail *nm* fan

éventé *a* (of beer) stale

évier *nm* kitchen sink

éviscérer *vt* (of meat) to draw, to eviscerate

excelsior *nm* cow's milk cheese; *a* fondant potato/braised lettuce-garnished

exhausteur de goût *nm* taste-enhancer

exocet *nm* sea fish: flying fish variety

exotique *a* (of cuisine) specialist, nation-oriented

explorateur *nm* soft cow's milk cheese

express *nm* espresso (expresso), squeezed-out

exprimer *vt* to press out the juice

exquis *a* exquisite, delicious, delectable

extra dry *a* (of champagne) less dry than brut

extrait *nm* extract, essence

F

fabada *nm* bean stew

façon *nf* method, manner of, way

facture *nf* bill

facturette *nf* (of credit card) chit

fade *a* (of food) tasteless

faïence *nf* crockery

faim *nf* hunger

faîne *nf* beechnut

faisan (ane) *nm/f* pheasant

faisandeau *nm* young pheasant

faisander *vt* (of game birds, poultry) to hang; ~é *a* high

fait *a* (of cheese) ripe

falette *nf* baked mutton breast

falsifié *a* adulterated

fameux (euse) *a* (of food/wine) top-class

fanchonnette (fanchette) *nf* meringued-covered cream-filled patisserie; strawberry-creamed macaroon; nougat/

hazelnut confection

fanon *nm* (of beef) dewlap; (of horse) fetlock; (of turkey) wattle; (of whale) baleen

faon *nm* young deer

far breton *nm* prune tart

farce *nf* farce, stuffing; (of meat) forcemeat

farci *nm* cabbage-wrapped forcemeat

farcidure *nf* poached forcemeat or vegetables

farcir *vt* to stuff

farée *nm* bacon or sorrel-stuffed cabbage stew

farinacé *a* farinaceous

farinage *nm* flour-based dish

farine *nf* flour; **~ complète** graham flour, coarse wholemeal; **~ de manioc** cassava; **~ pour gâteaux** self-raising flour

farinette *nf* small dice; pancake

farineux *a* floury, mealy, chalky, powdery, starchy

farlouche *nf* raisin/molasses pie mix

fatras *nm* gallimaufry, hash of left-over minced meat

faubonne *a* (of soup) haricot/vegetables/chervil-including

faugères *nm* Languedoc red wine

fausset *nm* (of barrel) bung, spigot, tap

faux col *nm* (of beer) head

faux mousseron *nm* fairy ring mushroom

faux-filet *nm* sirloin, tenderloin

favart *a* (of tarragon-ed poultry quenelles) Favart, mushroom/crayfish creamed garnished

favorite (à la) *a* (of soup) asparagus/lettuce; (of meat) asparagus-garnished, artichoke/celery/potato-garnished

favouille *nf* small green crab

fécond *a* fertile

fécule *nf* starch

féculent *a* starchy

fédora *a* chestnut/orange/asparagus/carrot-garnished

feijoa *nm* feijoa fruit; pineapple guava

femelle *a/nf* (of animals/plants) female; hen bird

fendant (chasselas) *nm* Swiss dry white wine; white wine grape variety

fenouil *nm* fennel; **~ bâtard** dill

fenugrec *nm* fenugreek, curry powder ingredient

féra *nf* Lake Geneva white fish: schelly (skelly)

ferchuse *nf* wine-casseroled pig's offal

férié (jour) *a* public holiday

ferme *nf* farm; *a* (of fruit) firm; (of poultry) free-range; (of meat) tough

fermé *a* shut

fermentation *nf* fermentation

fermenté *a* (of cheese) fermented

fermer *vt* to shut

fermette *nf* small farm

fermeture *nf* (of game season) close

fermière *a* of the farmer's wife, *usu* casseroled; **beurre fermier** dairy butter

ferval *a* artichoke-heart/croquette-potato/ham-garnished

festin *nm* feast

festonner *vi* to decorate in garlands

festoyer *vi* to feast

feta *nm* feta, brine-stored ewe or goat cheese

fête *nf* feast, holiday (extra-early booking advised! - *ed*)

fettucine *nf* fettucine, ribbon pasta

feu *nm* fire, burner, ring; **~ de bois** wood/peat fire; (of crockery) **au ~** ovenproof

feuillantine *nf* prune or apple patisserie

feuille *nf* leaf, vine leaf; **~ d'automne** meringue/chocolate mousse cake; **~ de dreux** cow's milk cheese

feuillet *nm* tripe

feuilleté *a* (of pastry) turned and rolled, flaky, puff; *nm* canapé, pastry

feuilleton *nm* stewed layered veal/pork with forcemeat

fève *nf* broad bean

fiasque *nf* glass straw-clad wine bottle

fiatole *nf* Mediterranean sea fish: stromateus fiatola: butterfish

fibre *nf* bulk, **~s** fibre

ficelle *nf* string; (of bread) stick; **~ picarde** cheese/ham/mushroom pancake

figer *vi* (of oil &c) to congeal

figue *nf* fig; **~ de barbarie** prickly pear; (of fish) **~ de mer** sea squirt, violet

figuette *nf* fig/juniper berry drink

fil dentaire *nm* dental floss

filandreux (euse) *a* (of meat &c) stringy

filbert *nf* aveline, hazel nut

filet *nm* fillet, tenderloin; **faux-~** sirloin; **~ de saxe** smoked salted pork; trickle of liquid

filo *a* (of pastry) filo (phyllo), flaky pastry

filtrat *nm* filtrate, filtered liquid

filtre *nm* filter; (of cigarettes) **bout ~** filter-tip; **~ à café** coffee filter

fin (fine) *a* thin; (of wine/food) fine, delicate, top quality, finest, finely-chopped; **~es herbes** mixed herbs

fin *nm* end; **~ de série** (of wine) bin end

finage *nm* (of wine) parish

financier *nm* creamy egg/almond patisserie

financière (à la) *a* sauced cockscomb/chicken/mushroom/truffle/Madeira garnished

fine *nf* (of wine) brandy; **~ champagne** top quality cognac; **~s de claire** oyster variety; **~s herbes** mixed herbs

finte *nf* sea fish: twaite shad (female)

fiore sardo *nm* soft ewe's milk cheese

fitou *nm* Languedoc wine

fixe *a* fixed

fixin *nm* burgundy wine

flageolet *nm* flageolet bean, Lima bean

flamand *a* flemish

flamande (à la) *a* cabbage/ carrot/turnip/potato-garnished; *(usu)* beef hot-pot; (of asparagus) with sieved egg-yolk

flambé *a* flambé, set alight

flamiche (flamique) *nf* cheese or vegetable tart

flammenküche *nf* onion/cream/ bacon tart

flammuline à pied velouté *nf* mushroom variety: velvet stem, winter fungus

flamri (flamery) *nf* red fruit-covered wine-cooked semolina

flan *nm* custard tart; **~ au fromage blanc** cheesecake

flanc *nm* flank, side

flanchet *nm* (of beef) flank, side

flanquer *vt* to flank

flasque *nf* flask

flaugnarde (flangnarde) (flognarde) (flougnarde) *nm* brandied cinnamon fruit flan

flèche *nf* (of bacon) flitch, side

flet *nm* flounder

flétan *nm* halibut

fleur *nf* flower; white flour; **~ de (du) maquis** goat cheese

fleurer *vt* to dust work surface with flour

fleuri *nm* beaujolais wine

fleuriste (à la) *a* stuffed-tomato/ château potato-garnished

fleuron *nm* fleuron, puff pastry garnish for fish

flocons d'avoine *nmpl* rolled oats, porridge; **~ de maïs** cornflakes

florentin *a* Florentine; accompanied by spinach; **~s** thin chocolate

florian *a* braised-lettuce/onion/ carrot/potato-garnished

flottant *a* floating

floute *nm* potato-cake

fluide *a* fluid

flûte *nf* long french loaf; (of glass) flute

foie *nm* liver; **~ gras** (of goose/ duck) liver usually made into pâté; **~ de volaille** chicken liver

foin *nm* (of artichoke) choke

folie *nf* of various unusual ingredients

folle blanche (gros-plant *nm)* *nf* white wine grape variety

foncé *a* (of orange) burnt

foncer *vt* (of liquids) to darken

fond *nm* base, foundation; (of artichoke) heart; (for meat) reduced cooking-liquid/stock

fondant *nm* fondant, centre of chocolate creams; *a* melting, mellow

fondre *vt* to melt; **faire ~** to render

fonds *nm* stock

fondu *a* melted

fondue *nf* fondue; **~ savoyarde** (of cheese) deep-fried cheese, fondue; **~ bourguignonne** (of beef) deep-fried pieces variously-sauced; (of cheese) processed

fontainebleau *nm* soft cow's milk cheese

fontanges *nf* (of soup) Fontanges, sorrel-ed chervil-ed creamed pea soup

fontenelle (à la) *a* (of dish) egg-asparagus

fontina *nm* cow's milk cheese

forestière (à la) *a* mushroom-garnished

forêt *nf* forest; (of gateau) **~-noire** Black Forest

forme d'ambert *nm* blue cheese

fort *a* (of wine &c) strong

fou (folle) *a* wild

fouace (fouasse) (fougasse) *nf* flavoured pastry

foudre *nm* tun

fouet *nm* whisk; swizzle-stick

fouetter *vt* to whip

fougasse *nf* bread pancake

fougère *nf* fern

fougeru *nm* soft cow's milk cheese

four (petit) *nm* petit four, post-prandial cake/biscuit, mouthful

four *nm* oven; (of food) **au ~** baked

fourchette *nf* fork; **~ à découper** carving fork; (of poultry) wishbone

fourme *nf* cow's milk cheese variety *(usu* blue)

fournisseur *nm* provisioner, supplier

fourré *a* (of cake) sandwiched, filled; (of confectionery) chocolate creamed; **biscuit ~** custard cream

fourrer *vt* (of cakes &c) to fill; (of poultry) to stuff

foyer *nm* foyer, antechamber, vestibule

fraîcheur *nf* coolness

frais (fraîche) *a* fresh, not-stale, not-frozen

fraise *nf* strawberry; **~ de bois** wild strawberries; **~ de veau** veal intestine

fraisier *nm* strawberry plant; kirsch-flavoured creamed strawberry sponge

framboise *nf* raspberry, raspberry syrup, raspberry liqueur

framboise de logan *nf* loganberry

framboisier *nm* raspberry cake

français *a* french

française (à la) *a* hollandaise braised lettuce/asparagus/ potato-garnished

Francfort *nf* (of sausage) frankfurter

francillon *nf* potato/mussels/ celery/truffle salad

frangipane *nf* frangipane, almond pastry cream

frappé *a* iced, frappé

freezer *nm* freezer

frelaté *a* adulterated

frémir *vi* to simmer

frénette *nf* frénette, fermented ash-leaf drink

freneuse *nf* creamed turnip/ potato soup

fréquenté *a* frequented; well thought-of

fressure *nf* fry; pluck, heart/liver/ lungs

fretin *nm* (of fish) fry

freux *nm* rook

friable *a* friable, crumbly

friand *nm* filled puff pastry

friandise *nf* confection, delicacy, titbit

fribourg *nm* gruyère cheese

fricadelle *nf* fricadelle, fried small balls of minced meat

fricandeau *nm* fricandeau, braised fillet of veal

fricassée *nf* fricassée, white sauce stew

frigidaire® *nm* fridge

frinault *nm* cow's milk cheese

frire *vt* to fry

frisé *a* **chou ~** kale (kail)

frit (frite) *a* fried

fritelle *nf* sausage or cheese or vegetable fritter

frites *nfpl* chips, French fries, fries

fritons *nm* crisp Auverge pork; pork/offal rillette

fritot (friteau) *nm* savoury tomato-sauced fritter of various ingredients

fritto misto *nm* savoury fritter of various ingredients

friture *nf* (of food) deep-fried; **petite ~** whitebait

froid *a* cold; **viande ~e** cooked cold meats

fromage *nm* cheese; **~ blanc** soft white cheese; **flan au ~ blanc** cheesecake; **~ frais** fromage frais, fresh creamy cheese; **~ gras** full-fat cheese; **~ de tête** brawn

fronsac *nm* Libournais red wine

frontignan *nm* Hérault wine

fronton *nm* Tarn/Garonne wine

frottis *nm* creamy herbed/ (cheesed) paste

frugal *a* frugal, abstemious

fruit *nm* fruit; **~s confits** glacé fruit; **~ de la passion** passion-fruit; **~ déguisés** marzipan-filled; **~s rafraîchis** (of fruit salad) alcohol-including; **~s de mer** seafood

fruité *a* fruity, fruit-flavoured

frumenty *nm* spiced porridge

fruste *a* (of food) coarse

fumé *a* smoked

fumer *vt* to smoke, to cure

fumet *nm* aroma, bouquet; reduced cooking-liquid/stock

fusion *nf* blend

fût *nm* barrel, cask

futaille *nf* cider barrel

G

gaillac *nm* south-west France wine

galanga *nm* galangal spice

galantine *nf* galantine, cold farced glazed white meat; cold stuffed bird

galet *nm* sea fish: bream

galette *nf* puff pastry base; **~ à l'avoine** flapjack, oatcake; **~ des rois** marzipan-filled puff pastry

galia *a* melon variety

galicien *nm* pistachio cream sponge cake

galimafrée *nf* gallimaufry, badly-cooked dish

galinette *nf* sea fish: gurnard

gamay *nm* red wine grape variety

gamba *nf* Mediterranean prawn

ganache *nf* ganache (a cream)

gaperon (gapron) *nm* cow's milk cheese

garage *nm* garage

garbure *nf* garbure; vegetable purée soup; vegetable/goose stew

garçon *nm* waiter

garde-chasse *nm* gamekeeper

garde-manger *nm* larder, meat-safe

gardon *nm* freshwater fish: roach

garenne (de) *nm* (of rabbit) wild

garnir *vt* to garnish, to dress, to serve with

garniture *nf* garnish, accompaniment, filling, fixings, trimmings; **~ de table** cruet

gaspacho *nm* gaspacho; cold spiced vegetable soup

gastrique *nf* reduced sugar/vinegar

gastronome *nf* epicure, gastronome, **à la ~** pot roasted stuffed-chicken/truffles/chestnut cockscombs/kidneys-garnished; sautée potatoes truffle-garnished

gastronomique *a* epicurean, gastronomic

gâte-sauce *nm* scullion, dish-washing hand

gâteau *nm* cake, patisserie, pastry, tart; **~ d'algues** laverbread; **~ d'anniversaire** birthday cake; **petit gâteau sec** biscuit; **~ de savoie** sponge cake

gâter (se) *vtr* (of food) to go bad

gaterin *nm* Mediterranean sea fish: haemulidae: grunts

gâtis *nf* cheese brioche

gaude *nf* reseda; **~s** cornmeal porridge

gaufre *nf* waffle; **~ en cire** honeycomb

gaufrette *nf* wafer

gauloise (à la) *a* coxcombs/kidneys-including; (of fish) crayfish/creamed-mushroom/truffles-garnished

gavage *nm* (of geese) fattening, forced-feeding

gave *nm* Pyrenees stream

gaz carbonique *nm* carbon dioxide

gaz *nm* gas

gazelle *nf* gazelle

gazeux (euse) *a* fizzy, aerated, effervescent

gazinière *nf* gas cooker

gefilte *a* gefilte, moussed, stuffed

gélatine *nf* gelatine, isinglass

gelé *a* frozen

gelée *nf* jelly, aspic; **~ royale** royal jelly

gélifiant *nm* jelly-ing agent

gélinotte *nf* hazel grouse

gélose *nf* agar-agar, stabilising/ thickening agent

gemme *a* (of salt) rock

gendarme *nm* pickled herring; beef sausage

génépi *nm* genepi, wormwood; absinthe liqueur

généreux *a* generous, (of wine) rich, full-bodied

génétique *a* genetic, **manipulation ~** genetic engineering

genevoise (à la) *a* genoese; genevoise-sauced; fish-liquid/ mirepoix/red wine-sauced

genièvre *nm* juniper, gin, geneva

génisse *nf* heifer

génois *a* genoese; sponge cake

génoise *nf* small sponge cake with soft creamed butter

gentiane *nf* gentian

gérant (e) *nm/f* (of restaurant) manager (esse)

germe *nm* (of grain) germ, shoot;

~ de soja beanshoot

germiny *nm* sorrel/spinach soup

germon (thon blanc) *nm* long-finned tuna

gésier *nm* gizzard

get *nm* mint liqueur

gewürztraminer *nm* white Alsace grape variety

ghee *nm* ghee, clarified butter/fat

ghivetch *nm* meat/vegetable/ yoghurt stew

gianduja *nm* chocolated crushed nuts

gibelotte *nf* savoury stew of rabbit/bacon/onion

gibier *nm* game; **~ d'eau** waterfowl

giclée *nf* (of soda-water) splash

gigolette *nf* (of fowl) leg

gigondas *nm* Rhone wine

gigot *nm* leg, haunch; slice from the leg or haunch

gigue *nf* leg, haunch

gimblette *nf* almond/citron-zest crown-shaped biscuit

gueuleton *nm* blow-out

gin *nm* gin; **~-tonic** gin and tonic; **cocktail de ~ et d'angusture** pink gin

gingembre *nm* ginger; **boisson gazeuse au ~** gingerbeer

ginseng *nm* ginseng

giraumon *nm* gourd

giraumonade *nf* pumpkin purée; ratatouille-ingredient

girelle *nf* girella fish; **~ royale** male girella

girofle (clou de) *nm* clove

girolle *nf* chanterelle mushroom

gîte *nm* (of beef) leg; **~-~** shin

givré *a* frosted, sprinkled; (of sorbet) in orange skin

givry *nm* burgundy wine

glaçage *nm* icing, frosting

glace *nf* ice, ice cream, icing; **~ à la crème** dairy ice; **pince à ~** ice-tongs; **seau à ~** ice-bucket; **~ portative** ice-cream gâteau; (of meat) glaze

glacé *a* glacé, crystallised, iced

glacière *nf* cool-box, cooler, ice-box

glaçon *nm* ice-cube

glissant *a* (of fish) slippery

glouton (onne) *nm/f* glutton

glucose *nm* glucose

gluten *nm* gluten

glycérine *nf* glycerine

gnocchi *nmpl* gnocchi, sauced dumplings

gobelet *nm* goblet, beaker, mug

gober *vt* (of oyster) to swallow whole

gobie *nm* sea fish: goby

godard *a* quenelle/sweetbread/coxcomb/kidney/mushroom-garnished

godiveau *nm* forcemeat of veal or fish

goéland *nm* gull

gogue *nf* blood sausage

golfe *nm* bay, gulf

gombo *nm* okra, gumbo; **~ filé** gombo soup; spicy chicken or seafood soup

gomme arabique *nf* gum arabic

goret *nm* porker

gorge *nf* throat; (of bird) breast; **~-de-pigeon** cherry variety

gorgette *a* georgette, Nantua-sauced crayfish tail-garnished; (of pancakes) apricot/pineapple/rum-garnished

gorgonzola *nm* gorgonzola, soft blue cow's milk cheese

gouda *nm* cow's milk cheese

gougère *nf* cheese-flavoured savoury choux

goujon *nm* gudgeon; small fillet; **~ de mer** (of sea fish) goby fish; (of freshwater fish) gudgeon

goujonnette *nm* young gudgeon, goujon; narrow strips of deep-fried fish fillet; flathead catfish

goulache (gulyas) *nf* goulash, spicy meat/onion stew

goulot *nm* (of bottle) neck

goumi *nm* goumi berry

gourde *nf* calabash, gourd, squash

gourgane *nf* large broad bean variety

gourmand *a* of fine food; gluttonous; *nm* gourmand, appreciator of fine food

gourmet *nm* epicure, gourmet

gournay *nm* cow's milk cheese

gousse *nf* pod, (of garlic) clove; **légume à ~** pulse

goût *nm* taste, liking, flavour

goûter dînatoir *nm* high tea

goûteux (euse) *a* tasty, full of flavour

goutte *nf* drop, nip, dram
gouttelette *nf* driblet, droplet
goyave *nf* guava
goyère *nf* cheese flan
gozette *nf* cinnamon-ed apple pastry
grâces *nfpl* grace (after meal)
gradin *nm* plinth
gradué *a* (of jug) measuring
grain *nm* grain; **de ~** corn-fed; **alcool de ~** grain alcohol; **~ de café** coffee bean; **poivre en ~s** peppercorns
graine *nf* seed
graisse *nf* dripping, fat, raw-meat fat, grease; **~ de rognon** suet
grammont *nm* (of lobster/ crayfish) layered dressed-meat/ meat/oysters
gramolate *nf* sorbet
grand veneur *a* (of ground game) redcurrant cream-sauced
grand mère *a* homely casserole-cooked
grand duc *a* grand-duc, asparagus/truffle-garnished
Grand Marnier *nm* Grand Marnier®, orange liqueur
granita *nf* ice-cream variety
granité *nm* granular sorbet
granule *nm* granule
grappa *nf* marc, grape-residue brandy
grappe *nf* (of grapes) bunch
gras *nm* raw- or cooked-meat fat, blubber; *a* fatty, oily; **~-double** tripe dish; **matière ~se**

shortening; **fromage ~** full-fat cheese; **tranche ~se** silverside
grataron *nm* goat cheese
gratin *nm* grated-cheese or crumbs-topped; **gratiné** *a* au gratin, crumbed/buttered/ cheesed
gratinée *nf* breaded cheesed onion soup au gratin
gratte paille *nm* cow's milk cheese
grattons *nmpl* cold meaty residue of pork/goose fat; crackling
gratuit *a* free
graveleux (euse) *a* (of fruit) gritty
gravlax (gravadlax) *nm* gravadlax, pickled raw salmon
gré *nm* liking, **au ~ des saisons** in season
grècque (à la) *a* Greek style; Mediterranean ingredients-influenced
grelot *nm* (of onion) pickling
grenache *nm* red grape variety
grenade *nf* pomegranate
grenadier *nm* sea fish: grenadier
grenadin *nm* grenadin, fricandeau of small rounds of veal
grenadine *nf* grenadine, pomegranate syrup
grenaille *nf* (of chicken) middlings
grenobloise (à la) *a* (of fish) meunière-cooked lemon/ capers-garnished
grenouille *nf* frog

grésiller *vi* to sizzle

gressin *nm* bread stick

greubons (grabons) *nmpl* residue from rendered pork fat

gribiche *a* (of sauce) hard-boiled egg-white herb-mayonnaised

griffe *nf* shoulder/neck beef cut; (of poultry) claw

gril *nm* (of utensils) grill, grill-pan

grill *nm* grill; carvery, grill-room

grillade *nf* grilled food

grillé *a* (of fish/meat) grilled, broiled; (of bread) toasted; (of coffee) roasted; **~ aux pommes** apple patisserie

grille-pain *nm* toaster

grillons (rillots) (rillauds) (rillons) *nmpl* residue from rendered pork fat; caramel-browned pork shoulder/belly

grilse *nm* grilse, young salmon

grimper *vt* to climb

griotte *nm* Morello cherry

griottine *nf* small cherry

gris (grise) *a* grey; (of pepper) black; (of wine) pale rosé; **~ de Lille** soft cow's milk cheese

griset *nm* sea fish: black bream

grisette *nf* mushroom variety: grisette

grissini *nm* grissini, crisp bread sticks

grive *nf* thrush

grog *nm* rum toddy, grog

gronau *nm* sea fish: gurnard

grondeur *nm* sea fish: bream-like variety

grondin *nm* gurnard, gurnet *(see rouget)*

gros (sse) *a* large, thick; **~sse cuillerée** heaped spoonful; (of noisette) cob nut; (of salt) coarse; **~-plant (folle blanche** *nf)* Nantes white wine grape variety

groseille rouge *nf* redcurrant; **~ à maquereau** gooseberry; **~ blanche** whitecurrant

grouse *nf* grouse

gruau *nm* gruel

grume *nf* grape

grumeau *nm* (of sauce, salt &c) lump

grumeleux *a* gritty

gruyère *nm* gruyère: hard cow's milk cheese

guacamole *nm* spicy avocado/tomato/onion/lemon juice dip

guêlon *nm* cream fruit-tart additive

gueuze *nm* beer

gui *nm* mistletoe

guide *nm* guidebook

guigne *nf* cherry variety

guignette *nf* open-air café

guignolet *nf* cherry liqueur

guillaret *nf* sweet pastry

guimauve *nf* marshmallow

H

habiller *vt* (of fish/fowl) to prepare pre-cooking; to dress

haché *a* minced, crushed; *nm* mince

hachée *nf* anchovy butter herbed

mushroom/shallot sauce

hacher *vt* to cut up, to chop up, to crush, to mince

hachis *nm* hachis, chopped vegetables, mince of vegetables, forcemeat; (of meat) mince

hachoir *nm* chopper, chopping-board, mincer

hachua *nm* braised fat ham/sirloin

haddock *nm* smoked haddock

haggis *nm* haggis, offal/onion/suet/oatmeal in sheep's stomach

halal *a* halal

halévy *a* (of poached egg, fish) double-sauced

halicot *nm* mutton stew

haliotide *nf* abalone, edible mollusc

halle *nf* covered market

halva *nm* halva, buttery sesame/nut sweetmeat

hamburger *nm* burger

hampe *nf* (of beef) flank, (of venison) breast

handicap physique *nm* physical handicap

hareng *nm* herring; **~ saur** smoked herring, kipper, bloater

haricot *nm* bean; **~ à rame** runner bean; **~ blanc** *nm* butter bean; **~ beurre** yellow french bean; **~ de soissons** kidney bean; **~ filet, aiguille** dwarf french bean; **~ mung** mung bean; **~ rouge** kidney bean; **~ vert** french bean; **~ à écosser** legume

harissa *nf* harissa; (of sauce) hot chilli

hase *nf* (of hare) doe

hâtelet (attelette) *nm* ornamental skewer

haut-pitou *nm* Vienne wine

haute cuisine *nf* haute cuisine

havane *nm* havana cigar

havir *vt* to sear, to seal; **havi** burnt-outside/raw-inside

helder *a* sautéed meat pieces potato/tomato sauce-garnished

Henri IV *a* grilled or sautéed meat or kidneys béarnaise/pont-neuf potato-garnished

herbes *nmpl* herbs; **fines ~, herbe à tortue** mixed herbs

hérisson *nm* hedgehog

hermétique *a* hermetic, air-/water-tight

hermitage *nm* Rhone wine

herve *nm* cow's milk cheese

hier *adv* yesterday

hirondelles (soupe aux nids d') *nfpl* bird's nest soup

historer *vt* (of oranges &c) to cut ornamentally

hiver *nm* winter; **melon d'~** honeydew melon

hochepot *nm* hotchpotch; oxtail/vegetable stew

hollandaise *nf* hollandaise, rich hot butter/egg sauce

hollande *nm* dutch cheese

homard *nm* lobster

hominy *nm* dried maize kernel

homogène *a* (of sauce &c) smooth

hongroise (à la) *a* paprika-containing

hoplostète *nm* sea fish: orange roughy

hors d'oeuvre *nm* hors d'oeuvre, appetizer, starter; **~ au fromage** cheese cocktail-dip

Hospices de Beaune *nmpl* (of wine) made & sold by this charity

hostellerie *nf* hostelry

hot-dog *nm* hot-dog

hôtel *nm* hotel

hôtelier *nm* hotelier; (of sauce) dry duxelles/lemon/parsley creamed butter

hôtelière (à la) *a* with hôtelier butter

hôtesse *nf* hostess

houblon *nm* hop

houmous (hoummos) *nm* houm(o)us (hummus), chick peas/sesame/garlic/lemon paste

hovasy maso *nm* spiced boiled beef

huche *nf* (of bread) large bin

huchon *nm* huchen (salmonidae fish)

huile *nf* oil; **~ d'arachide** groundnut, peanut; (of olive oil) **~ vierge** virgin, unrefined

huilier *nm* cruet, oil & vinegar

huître *nf* oyster

humecter *vt* to moisten

hure *nf* (of wild boar) head

hussarde (à la) *a* (of braised beef) stuffed eggplant/potato-garnished; (of sauce) espagnole sauce with tomato/shallot/horseradish/ham; (of garnish) tomato/puréed-onion and mushroom/puréed-spinach

hydne *nm* hydnum mushroom

hydromel *nm* mead

hygrophore *nm* hygrophorus mushroom

hypocalorique *a* low-calorie, slim-line

hysope *nf* hyssop

I

ibère *nm* iberian moss, irish sea moss, carrag(h)een

ide mélanote *nf* freshwater fish: golden orfe

igname *nf* yam

iguane *nm* iguana

île flottante *nf* floating island, caramel-ed custard creamed whipped egg-whites

imbiber *vt* to moisten with syrup/alcohol

imbriago *nm* sea fish: gurnard

imbriquer *vt* to inlay

impératrice (à la) *a* (of dessert) cream/crystallised fruit-ed rice

impériale *a* richly and variously garnished

importé *a* imported

inarbittate *nm* meat/spinach turnover

inciser *vt* to score, to cut, to

make an incision

incivulate *nm* meat/onion turnover

inclus *a* (of bill) included

incongelable *a* unfreezable

inconnu *nm* salmon variety

incorporer *nf* (of eggs &c) to incorporate, to fold-in, to mix-in

incrément *nm* increment

indien *nm* (of bread) chapatti

indienne (à la) *a* a curry-including and often rice

indigène *a* indigenous, native

indigestion *nf* indigestion

infiltration *nf* percolation

infusette *nf* (of tea/coffee) bag

infusion *nf* (of herbal tea) infusion; brew

ingrédient *nm* ingredient

insipide *a* tasteless, insipid, flavourless

instantané *a* instant

interdit *ptp of vt* (of smoking &c) not allowed, forbidden

interfolier *vt* to interleave

invitation *nf* invitation

inzuchatte *nm* meat/marrow turnover

iodé *nm* iodine

irouléguy *nm* Pays Basque wine

isard *nm* chamois, isard

issues *nfpl* (of carcasse) inedible parts; (of flour) bran

italien (ne) *a* Italian; **glace à l'~ne** soft ice-cream; **à l'~ne** mushroom/ham/herbs-sauced; macaroni-garnished

ivoire *a* with stock-enriched

suprême sauce

ivre *a* drunk, intoxicated

J

ja(c)que *nm* jackfruit

jabot *nm* (of bird) crop

jabugo *nm* Spanish dried ham

jalousie *nf* marzipan patisserie

jambe *nf* leg; **~ be bois** (of beef) shin, knuckle

jambon *nm* ham; **~ au torchon** top-class ham; **~ blanc**, **~ de Paris** boiled ham; **~ de Parme** Parma ham; **~ fumé** gammon, ham

jambonneau *nm* hand of pork, knuckle; stuffed chicken thigh

jambonnette *nf* pork-bacon charcuterie

japonaise (à la) *a* chinese artichoke-garnished

jaque *nm* jackfruit

jaquette *nf* morning coat

jardin *nm* garden

jardinière (à la) *a* garnished with fresh vegetables

jarre *nf* jar

jarret *nm* knuckle, shin, hock, shank

jars *nm* gander, male goose

jasnières *nm* Touraine white wine

jatte *nf* shallow bowl

jaune *a* yellow; *nm* (of egg) yolk; **vin ~** sherry-like wine

jéroboam *nm* jeroboam, large wine bottle four-times normal size

jessica *a* bone-marrow/ artichoke/shallot/morel/anna potato-garnished

jésuite *nm* frosted marzipan patisserie

jésus *nm* large pork sausage

jet d'eau *nm* water fountain

jeton *nm* slot-machine token

jeune *a* young; (of vines) *usu* non-appellation classified

jeûner *vt* to fast

jeunesse *nf* (of wine) young-age

joël *nm* small sea fish: sand smelt

jointoyer *vt* (of pastry &c) to smooth

joinville *a* (of sole fillets) positioned in circle; prawn/ mushroom/truffle/sauce-garnished; prawn-sauced; (of gâteau) raspberry jam-filled

jouchée *nf* fromage frais

joue *nf* cheek, chop

jour *nm* day

judic *a* braised lettuce/stuffed-tomato/potato-garnished

judru *nf* marc-ed pork sausage

juive (à la) *a* (of carp) braised; (of artichoke) breadcrumbed mint/garlic-stuffed

jujube *nm* jujube

julep *nm* julep

jules-verne *a* stuffed potato/ turnip/mushroom-garnished

juliénas *nm* beaujolais wine

julienne *nf* sea fish: ling; thinly sliced vegetable, consommé with this

jumeau *nm* (of beef) clod

jument *nf* mare

jurançon *nm* Pyrénées wine

jus *nm* juice, sauce, gravy

jussière *a* stuffed onion/braised-lettuce/potato-garnished

juteux (euse) *a* (of fruit) juicy

K

kaki *nm* persimmon

kangourou *nm* kangaroo

karité *nm* shea

kascher *a* kosher

kaskaval *nm* ewe's milk cheese

katshkawalj *nm* ewe's milk cheese

kébab *nm* kebab (kabob)

ketchup *nm* ketchup

kir *nm* kir, dry white wine/cassis

kirsch *nm* kirsch, wild cherry liqueur

kiwano *nm* kiwano fruit

kiwi *nm* Chinese gooseberry

knödel (knödl) (knoedel) *nm* dumpling

kouglof *nm* raisin-ed brioche

koulibiac *nm* coubiliac, fish or meat/cabbage pie

kriek *nf* cherried beer

kromeski (cromesqui) *nm* kromeski, bacon-wrapped creamed/battered meat; hot sweet or savoury salpicon hors d'oeuvre

kummel *nm* kümmel, caraway liqueur

kumquat *nm* kumquat

L

l'étoile *nm* jura wine
la clape *nm* languedoc wine
la bouille *nf* soft cow's milk cheese
laboratoire *nf* (of pastry-maker &c) preparation room
labre *nm* sea fish: wrasse variety
lac *nm* lake
laccaire *nm* laccaria mushrooms: deceivers
lactaire *nm* lactary mushroom: milk cap variety
ladoix-serrigny *nm* Beaune wine
lager *nf* lager
lagopède des Alpes *nm* ptarmigan; ~ **d'écosse** red grouse
laguiole *nm* cow's milk cheese
lait *nm* milk; ~ **cru** raw, unpasteurised; **chocolat au** ~ milk-chocolate; ~ **écrémé** skimmed milk; **petit-**~ whey; **oeufs au** ~ egg custard; ~ **de poule** milk egg flip; (of coffee) white
laitance (laite) *nf* milt (melt), soft roe
laitue *nf* lettuce; ~ **romaine** cos lettuce; ~ **pommée** cabbage lettuce; ~ **croquante** iceberg lettuce
lalande-de-pomerol *nm* claret
lamballe *nf* pea/tapioca soup; stuffed quail

lambic *nm* Lambic beer
lame *nf* slice, strip; (of knife) blade
lamelle *nf* sliver, slice, strip; (of mushroom) gill
lamnie *nf* porbeagle shark
lampris *nm* Mediterranean sea fish: opah
lamproie *nf* lamprey
lançon *nm* sand-eel
landaise (à la) *a* Bayonne ham/goose-fat/mushroom-prepared
langouste *nf* crayfish
langoustine *nf* Dublin Bay prawn, scampi
langres *nm* soft cow's milk cheese
langue *nf* tongue; ~-**de-boeuf** beefsteak mushroom; ~-**de-chat** langue-de-chat, thin flat biscuit
languedocienne (à la) *a* tomato/aubergine/cep-inclusive
lanière *nf* strip
lapereau *nm* young rabbit
lapin (e) *nm/f* rabbit, doe
laqué *a* lacquered; **canard** ~ Peking duck
lard *nm* bacon, fat
lardé *a* larded
lardon *nm* lardon, lardoon; strip of bacon for larding meat
larme *nf* drop
lasagne *nf* lasagne, flat pasta
laurier *nm* laurel, bay
lavabo *nm* wash-basin
lavallière (la vallière) *a* richly/variously-garnished

lavande *nf* lavender
lavaret *nm* freshwater fish: pollan; sea fish: schelly (skelly)
lave-vaisselle *nm* dishwasher
lavette *nf* dishwashing cloth
lavgnon *nm* mollusc
lèche-frite *nf* drip-pan, dripping pan
léger *a* slim-line
légume *nm* vegetable, ~ **à gousse** pulse
légumineuse *nf* legume, pod-bearing plant
lemon-grass *nm* lemon-grass
lentille *nf* lentil
lest *nm* bulk, roughage
levain *nm* leaven, fermentation agent
lever *vi* (of dough) to rise, to prove
levraut *nm* leveret
levroux *nm* goat cheese
levure *nf* yeast, baking powder, barm
lézard *nm* lizard
liaison *nf* liaison; (of liquid food) thickening
libre-service *nm* self-service
liche *nf* sea fish: scad variety, derbio
lie *nf* (of wine) dregs, sediment, lees, dead yeast; ~ **de vin** wine-coloured; **sur** ~ (of wine) aged on dead yeast
liège *nm* cork
liégeoise (à la) *a* alcohol/juniper berry-containing; (of coffee/chocolate ice-cream) with whipped cream
lier *vt* to thicken
lieu noir *nm* saithe, coal-fish, coley; ~ **jaune** pollack
lièvre *nm* hare
ligurienne (à la) *a* saffron risotto/potato/stuffed tomato-garnished
lilloise (à la) *a* of Lille; (of cabbage) puréed with apple/onion
limande *nf* small flat fish of flounder variety: dab
limande-sole *nf* lemon sole
limbourg *nm* soft cow's milk cheese
lime *nf* (of fruit) lime
limité *a* limited
limonade *nf* fizzy lemonade
limoner *vt* to wash off impurities
limousine (à la) *a* from Limousin; (of red cabbage) potato/chestnut-garnished; (of stuffed casserole chicken) bacon/chestnut-garnished; (of omelette) ham/potato-garnished
lingot *nm* white kidney bean
lingue *nf* sea fish: ling
liqueur *nf* strong alcoholic drink; liqueur
liquide *a* liquid, thin or runny; (of honey) clear; *nm* liquor
liquoreux (euse) *a* (of wine &c) syrupy
lirac *nm* Gard wine
lisette *nf* lisette seafish
lisse *a* melon type

listao *nm* tuna-family fish
listrac-médoc *nm* claret
litchie *nm* litchi (lychee)
litre *nm* litre
littorine *nf* winkle
livances *nfpl* jam pancakes
livarot *nm* cow's milk cheese
livèche *nf* lovage
livonienne *a* carrot/celery/ mushroom/onion-garnished; *nf* fish velouté sauce
livre *nf* one-pound in weight; **~ de cuisine** *nm* cookbook
livroux *nm* soft goat cheese
lobe *nm* part of heart/liver
loche *nf* river fish: loach; **~ de mer** sea fish: rockling
loganiza *nf* chorizo-like sausage
lollo *nf* small lettuce variety
lomo *nm* ham
lompe *nm* lumpsucker fish
long (gue) *a* long; (of sauce) thin
long drink *nm* long drink
longane *nm* longan fruit
longchamp *nf* pea soup
longe *nf* loin, fillet
lorette *a* (of beef) chicken/ asparagus/truffle-garnished; (of potato) cheese-flavoured; (of lettuce) beetroot/celeriac- garnished
Lorraine *nf* (of quiche) of Lorraine; **à la ~** Lorraine- influenced; bacon-gruyère- including; (of meat) red cabbage/wine/apple-garnished
lotte (lote) *nf* freshwater fish: burbot, ling; sea fish: angler, monkfish, devilfish
louche *nf* ladle
loukoum *nm* turkish delight
loup *nm* sea bass; **~ d'atlantique** wolf fish; **~ marin** seal; catfish, wolf-fish
loupiac *nm* Bordeaux sweet white wine
louvereau *nm* sea fish: luvar
louvine *nf* sea fish: sea-perch
luette *nf* uvula
lump (lompe) *nm* lumpfish
luxe *nm* luxury
luzerne *nf* alfalfa
lyonnais *a* of Lyons (famous gastronomic district) (applied to several dishes); **à la ~e** (of potato) sliced/sautéed with sautéed onion
lyre *nf* sea fish: piper

M

macaire *a* potato-caked
macaron *nm* macaroon
macaroni *nm* macaroni, tubular pasta; **~ au gratin** macaroni cheese
macédoine *nf* Macedonia; mixed large-dice fruit or vegetables hot or cold with sauce
macérer *vti* to macerate, to soak in liquid, to marinade, to pickle
mâche *nf* corn salad, lamb's lettuce
mâcher *vt* to chew
machine *nf* machine
mâchon *nm* traditional Lyons

restaurant

macis *nm* mace

macle (macre) *nf* water chestnut

mâcon *nm* burgundy wine

mâconnais *nm* goat cheese

mâconnaise (à la) *a* wine-cooked dish onion/mushroom/shrimp/croûtons-garnished

macreuse *nf* (of beef) shoulder

mactre *nf* mactre, clam-like shellfish, surf clam

macvin *nm* marc-wine liqueur

madame *nf* waitress

madeleine *nf* Madeleine; cake of genoese mixture; biscuit

mademoiselle *nf* waitress

madère *nf* (of wine, sauce, cake) Madeira

madiron (madiran) *nm* south-west France wine

madrilène (à la) *a* (of consommé) tomato/celery-flavoured

magistère *nm* strong consommé, aphrodisiac(!)

magnum *nm* magnum, double-bottle

magret *nm* fillet of duck

mahon *nm* cow's milk cheese

maigre *a* thin, weak, meagre; (of broth) clear; (of cheese) low fat; (of meat) lean, meatless; (of diet) lean; *nm* (of fish) meagre (sciaenidae)

maillota *a* carrot/turnip/onion/bean-garnished

maintenon *a* (of dish) mushroom/onion/béchamel-prepared

maïs *nm* maize, sweetcorn

maison *nf* home, house; **de la ~** restaurant-specific

maître d'hôtel *nm* head waiter, man in charge of restaurant and responsible for finishing certain table-side dishes; (of sauce) lemon/parsley butter

maître queux *nm* chef

makaire *nm* sea fish: marlin

mako (requin mako) *nm* shark sea fish: mako

malaga *nm* sweet fortified wine

malakoff *nm* (of cake) nut-containing; (of pastry) with crystallised fruit/ice-cream or Chantilly cream

malanga *nf* malanga, edible tuber variety

malard *nm* mallard duck

malaxer *vt* to make supple, to knead

malbec *nm* red wine grape variety

mâle *nm* (of game) buck, male

malibu *nf* coconut liqueur

malt *nm* malt; **single ~, pur ~** single malt whisky

maltais *nm* orange/almond petit four

maltaise (à la) *a* orange-based

malté *a* malted

maltose *nm* maltose

malvoisie *nm* malmsey; white wine grape variety

mamaliga *nm* corn broth

mamirolle *nm* cow's milk cheese

mancelle (à la) *a* of Le Mans

manche *nf* (of mutton) shin

manchette *nf* paper frill

manchon *nm* almond cream-filled petit four

mandarin *a* (of duck) mandarin

mandarine *nf* mandarin, tangerine

mandoline *nf* double adjustable-bladed knife; multi-bladed vegetable/egg slicer

mange-mêle *nm* ratatouille/bacon/coconut milk

mange-tout *nm* mange-tout, sugar pea

manger *vt* to eat

mangoustan *nm* mangosteen

mangue *nf* mango

manhattan *nm* whisky/vermouth/bitters/cointreau/lemon/cherry cocktail

manier *vt* (of ingredients) to homogenize

manière *nf* manner, fashion, way, style

manioc *nm* (of flour) cassava, manioc

manipulant *a* (of wine merchant) blender

manipulation *nf* manipulation; **~ génétique** genetic engineering

manne *nf* hamper

manqué *nm* hazel-nut/raisins/aniseed/crystallised-fruit/liqueured sponge cake

manseng *nm* grape variety

mante *nf* devilfish

maquée *nf* cow's milk cheese

maquereau *nm* mackerel

maraîcher (ère) *a* (of produce) market garden

maranges *nm* burgundy wine

marasme d'oréade *nm* fairy ring mushroom

marasquin *nm* maraschino, wild black cherry liqueur

marbrade *nf* aspic-ed pig's head

marbré *a* marbled

marc *nm* marc, grape-residue brandy

marcassin *nm* young wild boar

marcelin *nm* strawberry jam/almond pâtisserie

marché *nm* market, **~ commun** Common Market

marcillac *nm* south-west France wine

mardi gras *nm* mardi gras, Shrove Tuesday, pancake day

maréchal *a* (of fish) white wine-poached with tomato/mushrooms; (of meat) truffle/asparagus/chateaubriand sauce-garnished

maredsous *nm* cow's milk cheese

marée *nf* market-sold fish/shellfish

marengo *a* Marengo, (of white meat) oil/wine/garlic-embellished

marenne *nf* oyster variety

mareyeur (euse) *nm/f* wholesale fishmonger

margarine *nf* margarine

margaux *nm* claret

Marguerite nf marguerite

mari vaux a parmesan-ed béchamel-ed french bean/carrot/potato/celery/artichoke-heart/mushroom-garnished

marie-brizard® nf aniseed liqueur

marie-louise a artichoke-heart/mushroom/onion-garnished; carrot/peas/turnip-filled tart

marignan nm apricot meringue savarin cake

marigny a french bean/peas/potato-garnished; artichoke-heart/creamed-sweetcorn/potato-garnished; french bean/pea soup

marinade nf marinade, pickle, souse

mariné a marinaded, pickled, soused

marinière a (of shellfish) marinière, stewed in onion/wine/own juice

marivaux a parmesan-ed béchamel-ed vegetable-filled potato garnish

marjolaine nf marjoram

marlin nm marlin

marmelade nf stew of, compote, mish-mash; filling; **~ dieppoise** sea-fish soup; **~ d'oranges** marmalade

marmite nf marmite, earthenware cooking pot; **petite ~** individual meat stews

marmiton nm kitchen boy

marocaine (à la) a (of mutton noisettes) saffron/tomato-puréed green pepper/courgette/chicken-garnished

maroilles (marolles) nm cow's milk cheese

marque nf label, brand

marquise nf type of ice cream

marron nm chestnut; **~ glacé** crystallised chestnut

Marsala nm Marsala, fortified wine

marsanne nm grape variety

martini® nm martini; gin/vermouth

mascarpone nm soft cream cheese

mascotte nf rum/praline/cream sponge cake; **à la ~** a sauced artichoke hearts/potato/truffle-garnished

maskinongé nm maskinonge: pike variety fish

masquer vt to coat

massalé nm spice

masséna a poached marrow bone/artichoke heart-garnished

massenet a (of eggs) artichoke heart/asparagus-garnished; (of meat) artichoke heart/marrow bone/french bean-garnished

massepain nm marzipan

massillon nm kirsch/almond petit four

mastiquer vt to chew

matafan (matefaim) nf sweet or savoury thick pancake

maté nm maté, holly shrub beverage

matelote *nf* matelote; (of fish) with wine/onion sauce

matière grasse *nf* shortening; fat

matignon *a* vegetable mixture; breadcrumb-ed vegetable fondue-stuffed artichoke heart-garnished

maturation *nf* maturing, mellowing, ripening

maturité *nf* ripeness

mauresque *nf* aniseed-orgeat drink

maury *nm* Roussillon wine

mauve *nf* mallow

mauviette *nf* lark

mauzac *nm* south-west France grape variety

mayonnaise *nf* mayonnaise, cold egg-yolk/oil/vinegar sauce

mazagrin *nm* high conical pottery cup; stuffed mashed-potato case

mazarin *nm* layered praline/dacquoise cake

mazarine (à la) *a* rice/mushroom/artichoke-heart vegetable-stuffed garnished

méchoui *nm* (of lamb &c) whole barbecued animal

médaillon *nm* (of meat) round slice

médicis *a* (of béarnaised lamb/beef) artichoke-heart/potato/peas/carrot-garnished

mélange *nm* mixture, blend

mélasse *nf* treacle, molasses; ~ **raffinée** golden syrup

melba *a* Melba, raspberry/icing sugar sauce; (of meat) velouté-sauced mushrooms/chicken/stuffed tomato-garnished

méli-mélo *nm* assortment

mélisse *nf* lemon balm

melon *nm* melon; ~ **de bourgogne** white wine grape variety

ménage (de) *nm* home-made, ordinary

ménagère (à la) *a* housewife style, simple style

mendiant *nm* 4 dried fruits, almond/fig/hazel-nut/raisin; cinnamon-ed apple on moist fried-bread

menetou-salon *nm* Berry *usu* white wine

menthe *nf* mint; ~ **poivrée** peppermint; **pastille de ~** peppermint; **gros bonbon à la ~** bull's-eye; **[whisky] glacé à la ~** mint julep

mentonnaise (à la) *a* south of France-vegetabled

menu *nm* menu, meal; ~ **du jour** to-day's menu; ~ **gastronomique** gastronomic/gourmet menu; ~ **touristique** economy set-menu; *a* finely chopped

menu-droit *nm* grilled cream-marinated poultry fillet

mer *nf* sea

mercédès *a* braised lettuce/mushroom/tomato/potato-garnished; sherried chicken consommé

mercurey *nm* burgundy wine

merguez *nf* red pepper-ed beef sausage

meringue *nf* meringue, baked whipped-eggwhite/sugar often with cream

merise *nf* wild cherry

merlan *nm* whiting; (of beef) topside cut

merle *nm* blackbird

merlot *nm* red wine grape variety

merlu (merluche) *nm* hake, dried cod

merluchon *nm* small hake

mérou *nm* grouper, sea-perch

merveille *nf* deep-fried dough

mescal *nm* agave spirit

mesclun *nm* mixed green salad

mesure *nf* measure

méthode classique *nf* (of sparkling wine) champagne method

métis (isse) *a* cross-bred

mets *nm* food, dish, savoury

metton *nm* cooked skimmed milk cheese

meule *nf* millstone-shaped cheese

meunier *nm* mushroom variety: the miller

meunière *nf* miller's wife; **à la ~** *a* cooked in butter/parsley/lemon

meurette *nf* red wine sauce

meursault *nm* burgundy wine

meutrir *vt* (of fruit) to bruise

mexicaine (à la) *a* tomato/red pepper/aubergine-garnished

mi-chèvre *nm* (of cheese) part-goat part-cow's milk

mi-cru *a* half-raw, crunchy

mi-cuit *a* half-cooked

miche *nf* loaf

micro-ondes *nfpl* (of oven) microwave

mie *nf* (of bread) soft part; **sauce à la ~ de pain** bread sauce; **pain de ~** sandwich loaf

miel *nm* honey; **rayon de ~** honeycomb **~ liquide** clear honey

miette *nf* crumb, piece

mignon *nm* (of meat) fillet, mignon; truffle/peas-filled artichoke-heart accompaniment; **~ maroilles** cow's milk cheese

mignonette *nf* coarse white pepper

mignot *nm* cow's milk cheese

mijoter *vt* to cook slowly, to simmer

mikado *a* rice/curry/soy-influenced; (of sauce) tangerine-peel hollandaise

milan *nm* sea fish: gurnard

milanais *a* citrus almond-paste pastry; rum/raisin/aniseed apricot-covered sponge cake

milanaise (à la) *a* (of dish) parmesan/breadcrumb-fried

milandre *nm* shark variety

milk-shake *nm* milk shake

millas (millias) (millasse) *nm* sweet or savoury fried porridge

millefeuille *nm* mille-feuille, flaky

pastry, puff pastry; creamed
jam-ed flaky pastry

millésime *nm* (of wine) year of
vintage

millet *nm* millet

mimolette *nf* cow's milk cheese

mimosa *a* (of egg) mimosa; hors
d'oeuvre including chopped
egg yolk

minervois *nm* Languedoc wine

minestrone *nm* minestrone,
thick pasta or rice soup with
vegetable

minnéola *nm* minneola, thin-
skinned tangelo

minolette *nf* cow's milk cheese

minute *nf* (of e.g. steak) small
quickly-cooked

mique *nf* dumpling

mirabeau *a* olive/anchovy/
tarragon-sauced

mirabelle *nf* sharp plum; plum
brandy

mirepoix *nf* mirepoix; base (for
sauce) of diced root vegetables

mirliton *nm* almond-cream
pastry

miroton (mironton) *nm* miroton,
boiled beef and onion sauce

mischbrot *nm* rye bread

mistelle *nm* fortified grape juice

mititei *nf* chipolata

mitonner *vt* to simmer

mixer *nm* blender, liquidiser; *vt*
to blend

mode (à la) *a* of the region;
(of beef) veal/carrot/onion-
including

moderne (à la) *a* braised lettuce
or other vegetable-garnished

moelle *nf* bone marrow, pith,
core, medulla

moelleux (euse) *a* mellow,
smooth, creamy, moist; (of
wine) sweet

moïna *a* (of sole) creamed
mushroom/artichoke-garnished

moisson *nf* crop, harvest

moitié *nf* half

mojhette *nm* red bean

moka *nm* moka (mocha) coffee;
(of cream cake) with moka

molle *a* (of cheese) soft

mollet (ette) *nm* (of egg) soft-
boiled

mollusque *nm* mollusc (mollusk)

mombin *nm* mombin, spanish
plum, hog plum

monbazillac *nm* south-west
France sweet white wine

monder *vt* (of fruit &c) to peel
after scalding

monégasque (à la) *a* cold egg/
tomato/herb/mayonnaise hors
d'oeuvre

monopole *nm* (of vineyard)
single-producer-owned

monsieur *nm* waiter

mont-blanc *nm* cream-covered
vanilla-ed chestnut purée

mont-d'or *nm* goat cheese

mont-doré *a* (of mashed potato)
baked egg-yolk-ed/cheesed

montagny *nm* white burgundy

montbazon *a* mushroom/
quenelle/truffle/lamb's

sweetbread-garnished

monter *vt* to swell; to butter-enrich

montglas *a* filled with tongue/mushroom/truffled madeira sauce

montgolfière *nf* montgolfier; balloon

montlouis *nm* Touraine white wine

montmorency *a* sour cherry-including; (of meat) carrot/potato-stuffed artichoke heart-garnished

montpesier *a* (of meat) artichoke heart/asparagus/truffle/madeira sauce-garnished; (of sponge cake) almond/raisin/crystallised fruit-garnished

montrachet *nm* goat cheese; Beaune white wine

montravel *nm* Dordogne white wine

montreuil *a* (of meat) artichoke heart/peas/carrot-garnished; (of fish) white wine/shrimp-sauced

montrouge *a* mushroom-inclusive

montségur *nm* cow's milk cheese

moques *nm* cloved sugared pastry

morbier *nm* cow's milk cheese

morceau *nm* slice, piece, bit, lump

morgon *nm* beaujolais wine

morille *nf* mushroom variety: morel

mornay *a* (of sauce) cheesed béchamel

mortadelle *nf* mortadella; myrtle-berry sausage; large Italian sausage; luncheon meat

morte-saison *nf* off-season

morteau (de) *a* (of sausage) smoked

mortier *nm* mortar

morue *nf* cod; **jeune ~** scrod, young cod or haddock

moscovite (à la) *a* russia-influenced

Moselle *nf* Moselle, Mosel valley wine

mostelle *nf* sea fish: greater forkbeard

mothais *nf* goat cheese

mou (molle) *a* (of toffee) chewy; (of cheese &c) soft

mou *nm* lights, lungs

mouclade *a* (of mussels) à la marinière curry or saffron-flavoured

moudre *vt* (of pepper &c) to grind

mouette *nf* gull

mouflon *nm* wild sheep

mouillé *a* wet

mouillette *nf* finger of bread, 'soldier'

moule *nm* (of baking) mould; (of fish) mussel

moulin *nm* (of pepper, coffee) mill; **~-à-vent** beaujolais wine

mouliner *vt* to mince

moulis *nm* bordeaux wine

moulu *a* (of coffee) ground

mourvèdre *nm* red wine grape variety

moussaka *nf* moussaka, mincemeat with aubergine/tomato/cheese

mousse *nf* mousse; (of beer) head; **~ de fruits** fool

mousseline *nf* mousse; egg/cream sauce; **pommes ~** mashed potatoes

mousser *vi* (of liquids) to effervesce

mousseron *nm* field mushroom

mousseux (euse) *a* frothy; (of wine) sparkling

moût *nm* grape juice

moutarde *nf* mustard; **~ blanche** mustard (and cress)

moutardier *nm* mustard-pot

mouton *nm* mutton

mouvette *nf* flat wooden spoon

mozart *a* fried celery/potato-stuffed artichoke heart-garnished

mozzarella *nf* cow's milk cheese

müesli (müsli) *nm* muesli, granola

muffin *nm* muffin

muge *nm* mullet

muid *nm* hogshead

mulet *nm* grey mullet; mule

munster (munster-géromé) *nm* cow's milk cheese

mûr *a* ripe

murat *a* (of sole) artichoke heart-garnished

mûre *nf* blackberry; mulberry

murène *nf* moray eel

murol *nm* cow's milk cheese

muscadelle *nf* white wine grape variety

muscadet *nm* dry Loire white wine grape variety

muscat *nm* muscatel white wine grape variety

museau *nm* brawn

musette *nf* lunch-pack

mye *nf* mollusc variety: soft-shell clam

myrte *nm* myrtle

myrtille *nf* blueberry, bilberry (blaeberry), huckleberry, whortleberry

N

nabuchodonosor *nm* (of bottle) nebuchadnezzar, very large wine bottle, 20 times standard bottle

nage (à la) *nf* pot-boiled

nageoire *nf* (of fish) fin

nager *vi* (of food) to swim in [liquid]

nain (e) *a* (of poultry) bantam

nandou *nm* rhea, small ostrich-like bird

nanette *a* artichoke heart/mushroom/lettuce/truffle-garnished and chicken/marsala-sauced

nantais *a* from Nantes; **à la ~** white wine-sauced; *nm* cow's milk cheese; almond/crystallised fruit kirsch-ed cake

nantua *nf* Nantua; truffled

crayfish; (of sauce) crayfish bechamel

napolitaine *nf* almond/apricot cake with crystallised fruit; *a* (of ice cream) Neapolitan; **à la ~** (of spaghetti) cheesed/tomato-ed

nappage *nm* topping, covering, glaze

nappe *nf* tablecloth

napper *vt* to top with, to cover with

napperon *nm* table mat

nature *a* (of tea/coffee) without milk, black; (of omelette) plain; (of rice) boiled; (of spirits) neat; (of fruit) unsugared

naturel (elle) *a* natural, chemical-free, organic

navarin *nm* navarin, mutton stew

navet *nm* turnip

navette *nf* orange flower-watered patisserie; rape

nebuchadnezzar *nm* nebuchadnezzar, large wine bottle (20 ordinary bottles)

nectar *nm* nectar

nectarine *nf* nectarine

nèfle *nf* medlar; **~ d'amérique** sapodilla fruit

négociant (NM) *nm* (of wine) buying-maturing-bottling-selling merchant; **~ manipulant** buyer/blender

neige *nf* snow; whipped egg-white; sorbet; **~ carbonique** dry ice

nem *nm* small spring roll (far eastern)

nemours *a* potato/peas/carrot-garnished; (of fish) shrimp-sauced and quenelle mushroom-garnished; (of soup) potato/cream/egg-yolk/tapioca-containing

nesselrode *a* chestnut purée-containing

net *a* all included, all-in

neufchâtel *nm* cow's milk cream cheese

néva (à la) *a* (of stuffed chicken) white chaud-froid sauced

newburg *a* (of lobster) cream-sautéed

niçois *a* of Nice; with tomato/anchovy/black olive

nid *nm* nest; **~ d'abeille** honey/almond/cream brioche; **soupe aux ~s d'hirondelles** bird's nest soup

nigelle *nf* nigella

ninas *nm* small cigar

ninon *a* asparagus-ed potato/cockscomb/kidney velouté-garnished; (of salad) lettuce/orange segmented

niolo *nm* goat cheese

nivernaise (à la) *a* glazed carrot/onion-garnished

noël *nm* Christmas; **tartelette de ~** mince-pie

noir *a* black; **boudin ~** black pudding; **radis ~** horseradish

noisette *nf* knob, noisette; round steak; potato-balls; hazel nut, cob nut

noix *nf* walnut; **~ de coco** coconut; **~ de cajou** cashew nut; **~ de muscade** nutmeg

non-fumeur (euse) *a* no smoking

nonette *nf* spicy bun; biscuit

nonnat *nm* sea fish: transparent goby

nonpareille *nm* pickled caper; hundreds and thousands

non-vintage *a* (of wine) *usu* single vintage blend

noque (knepfle) *nf* quenelle

normand *a* from Normandy, **à la ~e** with cream/apples or cider

norvégienne (à la) *a* (of cold seafood) cucumber/smoked salmon-garnished; egg/shrimp mousse-garnished; anchovy-based soufflé or puff pastry

note *nf* bill

nougat *nm* nougat; sugar/nut sweet

nougatine *nf* nougatine, chocolate-covered nougat

nouilles *nfpl* noodles

nourrice *nf* baby-minder

nourrir *vt* to nourish

nourrissant *a* nutritious

nourriture *nf* food; diet

nouveau (nouvelle) *a* new

nouvelle cuisine *nf* simple cooking

nouzillards *nmpl* milk-cooked chestnuts

noyau *nm* fruit stone; fruit stone liqueur/brandy

noyer *vt* (of food/alcohol) to drown, to over-dilute

nulle *nf* musk-flavoured cream custard

numéro *nm* number

nutritif *a* nutrient

O

oblade *nf* saddled sea bream

obligatoire *a* compulsory

occident *nm* west

occupé *a* occupied

oeillette *nf* poppy variety

oeuf *nm* egg, roe; (of egg) **~ à la coque** boiled; **~ au plat** fried; **~ à la neige** floating island; **~ poché** poached; **~ poché Albert** poached egg on salmon-ed artichoke heart; **~ en cocotte** baked egg, shirred egg; **~ au lait** egg custard; **~s brouillés** scrambled eggs

oie *nf* goose

oignon *nm* onion; scallion; **petit ~** pickling onion

oiseau *nm* bird; **~ sans tête** stuffed rolled tied meat

oison *nm* gosling

okra *nm* okra

oléagineux *nmpl* (of nuts &c) oily/oleaginous fruit

olive *nf* olive; **~ de mer** shell-fish variety: small coquille saint-jacques

olivet *nm* cow's milk cheese; **~ cendré** cow's milk cheese

olivette *nf* plum tomato

omble (omble-chevalier) *nm*

sea fish: charr

ombre nm migratory fish: grayling

ombrine nf sea fish: meagre, ombrine

omelette nf omelette (omelet)

onctueux (euse) creamy, smooth

onglet nm (of beef) prime cut

opéra nm opera ice-cream

oranais nm apricot cream pastry

orange nf orange

orangeade nf orangeade

orangeat nm orange-candied almond petit four

ordinaire a (of wine) ordinary, everyday, plonk

oreille nf ear; (of saucepan) lug; ~ **de lièvre** lamb's lettuce

oreiller de la belle aurore nm rich game/meat pie

oreillette nf sweet pastry fritter

oreillon nm (of apricot &c) half

organique a organic

orge nf barley; **sucre d'~** (of confectionery) rock, candy

orgeat (sirop d') nm barleywater, orgeat

orientale (à l') a middle-east vegetables-containing

origan nm oregano

origine nf origin

orignal nm moose

orléanaise (à l') a endive/potato-garnished

orléans a (of egg) bone-marrow/truffle/madeira-sauced tomato-sauced/chicken-garnished; (of

sole) shrimp/mushroom/white wine-sauced

orloff a braised lettuce/celery/potato-garnished; (of veal) parmesan-ed mushroom/onion-sauced

orly a (of fish) battered/tomato-sauced

ormeau nm abalone, ormer, mollusc variety

orner vt to garnish, to ornament

oronge nf mushroom amanita variety: caesar's mushroom

orphie nf garfish

ortie nf nettle

ortolan nm ortolan, bunting

orval nf beer

os nm bone

oseille nf sorrel

ossau fermier nm cow's milk cheese

ossau iraty nm ewe's milk cheese

osso buco nm veal stew

ôter (les arêtes) vt (of fish) to bone

ouananiche nf freshwater salmon

ouassou nm freshwater crayfish

oublie nf wafer

ouïes nfpl (of fish) gills

oursin nm sea urchin

ourteto nm spinach/sorrel/celery/leek/garlic dish

outarde nf bustard

outil nm freshwater fish: houting

ouvert (te) a open

ouvre-boîtes nm tin- (can-)

opener

ouvre-bouteille *nm* bottle-opener

ouvre-huître *nm* oyster-opening knife

ouvrir *vt* to open

ouzo *nm* ouzo, aniseed spirit

ovin *a* ovine, sheep-like

oyonnade *nf* goose stew

P

pacane *nf* pecan nut

pachade *nf* fruit pancake

paella *nf* paella, garlic-ed spiced rice/shellfish/chicken/vegetable

pagel *nm* sea bream variety: pandora

pageot *nm* bream-family fish

pagre *nm* Mediterranean fish: sea bream (couch's sea)

paillasson *nm* mat, base

paille *nf* drinking straw; **pommes ~(s)** in thin strips; **vin de ~** wine from grapes dried on straw mats

paillette *nm* parmesan-ed petit four

pain *nm* bread; **arbre à ~** breadfruit tree; **~ au chocolat** chocolate-ed éclair; **~ azyme** unleavened; **~ bis** brown bread; **~ complet** wholemeal; **~ d'épice** spiced-bread, gingerbread; **~ de gêne** Genoa cake, almond sponge cake; **~ de ménage** cottage loaf; **~ de mie** sandwich loaf; **~ de**

seigle rye bread; **~ de sucre** sugarloaf; **~ indien** chapatti; **~ perdu** French toast; **petit ~** roll; **petit ~ au lait** bun; **pudding de ~** bread-and-butter pudding; **sauce à la mie de ~** bread-sauce; **~ de ménage** cottage loaf; **~ noir** pumpernickel

paire *nf* (of gamebirds) brace

palace *nm* five-star hotel

palée *nf* Swiss lake fish: schelly (skelly)

paleron *nm* chuck, cut of meat from neck to ribs

palet *nm* biscuit; **~ frais** goat cheese

paletot *nm* cardigan, casing

palette *nf* (of pork) shoulder

palme *nf* palm

palmier *nm* flaky-pastry biscuit

palois *nf* layered almond meringue

palombe *nf* woodpigeon

palomette (palomète) *nf* sea fish: plain bonito

palomine *nf* sea fish: derbio

palourde *nf* clam; **soupe de ~(s)** chowder

pamplemousse *nm* grapefruit

pampus argenté *nm* Mediterranean sea fish: black-fish variety

pan-bagnat *nm* onion/anchovy/celery/olive sandwich

panaché *a* mixed, mix-flavoured, assorted; (of beer) shandy

panade *nf* panade, panada, thickening; bread soup

panais *nm* parsnip

pané *a* (of breadcrumbs) coated with

paner *vt* to breadcrumb

panetière (à la) *a* in baked-bread case

panettone *nm* panettone, large spiced brioche

panier *nm* basket; **~ à salade** salad basket/shaker; **le dessus du ~** pick of the crop; **~-repas** lunch-basket, pack lunch; **petit ~** punnet

panification *nf* bread-making

panne *nf* pork kidney-encasing fat

pannequet *nm* pancake

panorama *nm* panorama, view

panse *nf* stomach

panure *nf* fresh breadcrumb

papaye *nf* papaya, pawpaw

papet *nm* leek/potato soup

papeton *nf* egg/aubergine purée

papier *nm* paper; **~ aluminium, ~ d'argent** tin foil; **~ paraffiné** greaseproof paper

papillote *nf* wrapper, foil, paper case, frill; (of confectionery) sweet in wrapper

paprika *nm* paprika

pâques *nfpl* Easter

paquet *nm* packet, parcel

paradis *nm* heaven, paradise

parfait *nm* parfait; mould of ice-cream with cream sauce/meringue/fruit/syrup; **~ amour** lemon/herb liqueur

parfum *nm* smell, aroma; flavour

parfumé *a* perfumed

paris-brest *nm* praline creamed almond pastry

parisien *nm* lemon/almond/crystallised-fruit/meringued sponge cake

parisienne (à la) *a* braised lettuce/potato/artichoke heart-garnished; (of cold seafood) mayonnaised; (of soup) leek/potato/chervil-ed

parking *nm* car park

parmentier *a* potato-containing; of chopped vegetables; (of meat) mince; **hachis ~** cottage pie; **potage ~** leek/potato soup

parmesan *nm* strong very hard cow's milk cheese

part *nf* (of cakes &c) finger, portion, slice

partage *nm* (of cake) cutting

pâs-d'ane *nm* coltsfoot

pascaline *a* (of lamb) stuffed and roasted whole

passer *vt* to strain

passetoutgrains *nm* (of burgundy) Gamay/Pinot Noir blend

passion *nf* (of fruit) passion

passoire *nf* (for liquids) sieve, strainer, colander

pasteles *nfpl* stuffed plantain leaves

pastenague *nf* skate variety: sting ray

pastèque *nf* watermelon

pasteuriser *vt* to pasteurise

pastilla *nf* pigeon or fish or

vegetable pie

pastillage *nm* gum sugar paste

pastille *nf* pastille, lozenge; **~ de chocolat** chocolate drop

pastirma *nm* dried salted meat

pastis *nm* pastis, aniseed spirit

patate *nf* sweet potato, yam

pâte *nf* pastry, pastry mixture, paste, cream, mix, spread; **~s** pasta; **~ à pain** dough; **~ brisée** shortcrust pastry; **~ sablée** sugarcrust; **~ à choux** choux pastry; **~ à crêpes** pancake-mix; **~ à frire** batter; (of cheese) cheese; **~ dure** hard; **~ molle** soft; **~ fermentée** fermented; (in soup) noodles; **~ d'amandes** marzipan; **~ de fruits** crystallised fruit, in jelly form; **~ de bécherel** garlic pie

pâté *nm* pâté, paste of meat; **~ de courres** gelatine of offal

pâtes *nfpl* pasta

pâtisserie *nf* pastry, cake, confectionery; pastry shop, patisserie

pâtisson *nm* squash

Patna *nf* (of rice) Patna, long thin grain rice

pâton *nm* (of bread) doughball

patron (onne) *nm* owner, proprietor

patte *nf* leg, paw, foot

patxaran *nm* sloe/aniseed liqueur

pauillac *nm* bordeaux red wine

paupiette *nf* (of veal or beef)

olive

pause-café *nf* morning coffee

pauvre *a* (of food) of little nutritional content; **à la ~ homme** sauced left-over meat

pavé *nm* thick steak; (of cake &c) slab; thick dry sausage; **~ d'auge** cow's milk cheese

pavin d'auvergne *nm* cow's milk cheese

pavot *nm* poppy

pays *nm* country, countryside, region, locality, village; **du ~** home-grown; (of wine) local, of the area

paysan (anne) *a* rustic; simple; peasant; braised with carrots/turnips/celery/onions

peau *nf* skin, peel, rind, down; **~ blanche** (of orange) pith; **~ bleu (requin bleu)** blue shark

pécan *nm* pecan

pécharmant *nm* south-west France red wine

pêche *nf* fishing; peach

pêcher *vt* to fish

pectine *nf* pectin

peigne (grand) *nm* coquille Saint-Jacques

pékinoise (à la) *a* (of fish) battered sweet and sour-sauced

pélagique *a* pelagic, deep-sea, open-sea

pélamide *nf* sea fish: bonito, pelamid

pélardon *nm* goat cheese

peler *vt* to remove superficial

layer

pèlerine (grande) *nf* coquille Saint-Jacques

pelle *nf* fish slice, scoop

pelote *nf* verni clam

pelure *nf* (of onion) skin

pemmican *nm* pemmican, dried cake of meat/berries

penchant *nm* taste (for), liking (of), addiction

penne *nf* pasta piece(s)

pépin *nm* pip, seed

pepino *nm* pepino fruit

pérail *nm* ewe's milk cheese

perchaude *nf* perch

perche *nf* sea/freshwater fish: perch

percolateur *nm* coffee percolator

perdreau *nm* young partridge

perdrix *nf* partridge

perdu *a* (of bread) French toast; (of dessert) bread-and-butter pudding; (of bottles/containers) disposable

périgourdin (ine) *a* from Périgord; containing truffles

Périgueux *a* from Périgueux; truffled madeira-sauced

périssable *a* perishable

perlant *a* slightly pétillant

perlé *a* slightly pétillant

perlon *nm* sea fish: gurnard

perroquet *nm* pastis/mint drink; **poisson ~** sea fish: parrot-fish

persane (à la) *a* (of lamb) aubergine/onion/tomato/ peppers-garnished

persil *nm* parsley

persillade *nf* parsley/garlic mix

persillé *a* chopped parsley-ed; (of cheese) blue-veined; (of beef) shoulder

persillée *nm* (of beef) top quality

pervenche *nf* periwinkle

peser *vt* to weigh

pessac-léognon *nm* bordeaux red or white wine

pesto *nm* pesto, pine-nut/basil/ garlic sauce

pet-de-nonne *nm* sweet fritter

pétale *nm* petal

pétillant *a* (of wine) lightly sparkling

petit (petite) *a* small; **~-beurre** shortbread; **~-four** petit four, small post-prandial cake/ biscuit, mouthful; **~ pain** bread roll; **~ salé** salted pork; **~e sirah** grape variety

petit déjeuner *nm* breakfast; **~ à l'anglaise** cooked breakfast

petit-duc *a* asparagus/truffle/ chicken purée tarts-garnished

petit-lait *nm* whey

petit verdot *nm* red grape variety

petit suisse *nm* cow's milk cream cheese

petite friture *nf* whitebait

pétoncle *nm* queen scallop, scallop

pétrir *vt* (of bread dough) to knead

phoque *nm* seal

photo *nf* photograph

physalis *nm* cape gooseberry

pibale *nf* freshwater fish: elver;

sea fish: young eel

pic *nm* (of ice) pick

picate *nf* sea fish: sea bass

picatta *nf* veal escalope

pichet *nm* blackjack, leather beer mug, wine jug

picholine *nf* pickled olive

pickles *nmpl* piccalilli

picodon *nm* soft goat cheese

picorer *vt* (of food) to pick at

picpoul-de-pinet *nm* Languedoc white wine

pièce *nf* piece, (of meat &c) slab; ~ **de résistance** (of dish) masterpiece, centrepiece; ~ **montée** ornamental patisserie piece; ~ **parée** (of beef) shoulder

pied *nm* foot, trotter; (of celery) stick or head; stem of a glass; ~**-bleu** wood blewits mushroom; ~ **de cheval** oyster; ~**s et paquets** sheep's trotters/ stuffed tripe

piémontaise (à la) *a* risotto-containing

pierre-qui-vire *nm* soft cow's milk cheese

pieuvre *nf* octopus

pigeon (eonne) *nm/f* pigeon

pigeonneau *nm* young pigeon, squab; young plump pigeon bred for table

pigne *nf* pine nut

pignon de pin *nm* pine kernel, nut

pigoulle *nf* cow or goat or ewe's milk cheese

pilaf(f) *nm* pilaf, pilau, kedgeree, boiled rice with meat or fish

pilchard *nm* pilchard

pilé *a* crushed; (of almonds) ground, pounded

pilon *nm* pestle, tool for crushing in mortar; (of fowl) bottom half of thigh

pilonner *vt* to crush

pils (pilsner) *nf* lager

pimbina *nm* pembina, cranberry-type

piment *nm* pimento, pepper (hot), capsicum, chili (chilli)

pimenté *a* spiced, with chilli

pince *nf* pincer, claw; (of ice, sugar) tongs

pinceau *nm* brush

pincée *nf* (of salt &c) pinch

pinot blanc/noir/gris *nm* varieties of grape

pintade *nf* guinea fowl

pintadeau *nm* young guinea fowl

pinte *nf* quart; pint

piochon *nm* green cabbage

piperade *nf* piperade, egged-peppers/tomato stew

piquant *a* hot, spicy, pungent, with bite, sharp

piqué *a* pitted with

pique-fruit *nm* cocktail stick

pique-nique *nm* picnic

piquer *vt* to lard, to introduce to the surface, to prick

piquette *nf* local (indifferent) wine, plonk

piscine *nf* swimming pool

pissaladière *nf* onion/anchovy

tart

pissalat *nf* spiced anchovy purée

pissenlit *nm* dandelion

pistache *nf* pistachio nut; *a* garlic-prepared

pistole *nf* pistole plum

pistolet *nm* breakfast roll

pistou *nm* (of soup) with basil/garlic; (of dessert) basil/oil/mint paste; oil/tarragon dressing; oil/mint dressing

pita *nm* pitta bread

pitahaya *nm* pitahaya cactus fruit

pithivier *nm* Pithivier cake; almond paste-filled

pizza *nf* pizza

placer *vt* (of guest/customer) to seat, to place

plaindre de (se) *vpr* to make a complaint about

plaisir *nm* wafer

planche *nf* (of bread) board

plantagenêt *a* cherry/cointreau-flavoured

plantain *nm* plantain

plaque *nf* plate, block, slab; ~ **chauffante** hotplate; ~ **de cuisson** hotplate; ~ **en fonte** griddle

plaquette *nf* (of chocolate &c) bar

plat *nm* dish, course; ~ **bourgeois** long-slow-cooked dish; ~ **cuisiné** (of meal) ready-cooked; ~ **d'accompagnement** side-dish; ~ **du jour** today's specials; ~ **garni** with vegetables; ~ **à feu** flame-proof dish; ~ **principal** main course; (of eggs) fried; (of beef) ~ **de côtes (dé)couvert** (un)covered rib

plat *a* (of fish variety) flat; (of beer) stale

plateau *nm* plateau, board, tray, mesa, salver

platée *nf* plateful

plein *a* full

pleurote *nf* oyster mushroom

pli *nm* section

plie *nf* plaice, witch

plier *vt* to fold

plombières *nf* kirsch-flavoured custard ice-cream

plonge *nf* dishwashing

pluche *nf* peeling; ~s heads of fresh herbs

plum-pudding *nm* fruit-cake

plumer *vt* (of birds) to pluck

pluvier *nm* tame plover, dotterel

poche à douille *nf* forcing-bag, piping-bag

pocher *vt* (of eggs) to poach

pocheteau *nm* skate

pocheuse *nf* (of eggs) poacher

pochon *nm* ladle

pochouse (pauchouse) *nf* freshwater fish soup; fish stew

poêle (poële) *nm* frying-pan, stove

poêlon *nm* pan, chafing dish, pipkin, skillet; dish with its portable fuel for table-side cooking

pogne *nf* fruit tart; large brioche

poids *nm* weight

poignée *nf* handful

poil *nm* hair, skin; (of artichoke) choke

point *nm* à ~ (of meat) medium cooked; (of fruit/cheese) ripe

pointe *nf* (of pork) top of leg; (of asparagus &c) tip

poire *nf* pear; (of beef) thigh

poiré *nm* perry, pear cider

poireau *nm* leek

pois *nm* pea; ~ **cassés** pease pudding; ~ **chiche** chickpea; ~ **gourmand** mange-tout

poisson *nm* fish; ~-**chat** *nm* freshwater fish: horned pout; ~**s d'eau douce** game fish, freshwater fish, coarse fish; ~-**écureuil** sea fish: sargocentron; ~-**pilote** pilot fish; ~ **salé** Bombay duck, dried fish; ~ **volant** sea fish: flying fish (several varieties); ~ **d'avril** 1st May fish-motif confectionery

poissonnière *nf* fish kettle

poitrine *nf* breast, brisket; (of pork) belly

poivrade *nf* peppered vinaigrette; piquant demi-glace sauce

poivre *nm* pepper; ~ **blanc** white pepper; **de cayenne** cayenne pepper; ~ **noir**, (~ **gris**) black pepper; ~ **en grain** peppercorns; ~ **vert** green pepper spice; **moulin à** ~ pepper-mill

poivrette *nf* nigella

poivrier (poivrière) *nm/f* pepperpot

poivron *nm* pepper (sweet), capsicum; ~ **rouge** red pepper

pojarsky *a* (of veal chops) fried; (of chicken breast/salmon) breaded and fried

polenta *nf* maize porridge

polignac *a* white-sauced truffled/ mushroom-ed

polka *nm* caramelised pastry-creamed patisserie

pollinisation croisée *nf* cross-pollination

polonaise (à la) *a* breadcrumbed cauliflower/aspapagus hard-boiled egg/parsley-garnished

polypore *nm* tree trunk-growing mushrooms

pomélo *nm* pomelo, shaddock, grapefruit

pomme *nf* apple; ~ **d'api** small apple variety; ~ **cannelle** custard apple; ~ **à couteau** eater, eating apple; ~ **à cuire** cooker, cooking apple; ~ **sauvage** crab-apple; (of lettuce) head

pommé *a* (of lettuce &c) firm/ round

pomme de terre *nf* potato; ~-**céleri** arracacia root

pompe *nf* sweet or savoury tart variously garnished

pondre *vi* (of birds) to lay

pont l'évêque *nm* cow's milk cheese

pont-neuf *nm* (of potato) thick

chips; (of pastry) jam/rum/ pastry cream-filled

pop-corn *nm* popcorn

poppadum *nm* poppadum (poppadam) (papadum), thin crisp spiced bread

porc *nm* pork

porcelaine *nf* porcelain; ~ **tendre** bone china

porcelet *nm* sucking pig

porée *nf* vegetable soup

porquerolles *nm* wine growing area

porridge *nm* porridge

port-salut *nm* cow's milk cheese

porte de secours *nf* emergency exit

porte-maillot *a* carrot/turnip/ onion/bean-garnished

portefeuille *nm* wallet

portemanteau *nm* coat-rack (coat-stand)

portier *nm* doorman

portion *nf* helping, portion

porto *nm* port wine

portugaise (à la) *a* tomato-influenced

pot *nm* pot; Lyon 45cl bottle; ~ **de grès** stoneware pot

pot-au-feu *nm* deep earthenware casserole; (of beef) stew

potable *a* drinkable

potage *nm* soup; ~ **parmentier** leek/potato soup

potager (~ère) *a* edible, vegetable; *nm* kitchen garden; **herbes ~ères** potherbs

potagère *nf* lamb's lettuce

potée *nf* earthenware-pot stew

poterie *nf* crockery

potima(r)ron *nm* chinese okra

potiron *nm* large pumpkin

potjevlesch *nf* 3-meat terrine

pouce-pied *nm* goose barnacle

poudre *nf* powder; (of eggs &c) **en ~** dehydrated, instant; **chocolat en ~** drinking chocolate

poulamon *nm* poulamon fish

poularde *nf* fatted chicken

poule *nf* chicken; ~ **au pot** stewed stuffed chicken with beef; ~ **d'eau** moorhen; **lait de ~** milk egg flip

poulet *nm* broiler, chicken; ~ **de grain** corn-fed chicken; ~ **fermier** free-range chicken

poulette *nf* pullet, young domestic fowl; velouté sauce egg/lemon/parsley-finished

pouligny-saint-pierre *nm* goat cheese

poulpe *nm* octopus

poumon *nm* lung, lights

pounti *nm* casseroled bacon hash/onion/swiss chard

poupelin *nm* whipped-cream or ice-cream-filled patisserie

pouponnière *nf* crèche

pourboire *nm* tip

pourceau (grand) *nm* sea bass; pig

pourly *nm* goat cheese

pourpier *nm* portulaca plant

pourri *a* decayed, rotted; (of egg) addled

pousse *nf* (of bamboo &c) shoot

pousse-café *nm (slang)* post-prandial spirits

poussin *nm* young bird; 4-6 week old chicken

poutargue (boutargue) *nf* botargo, salted pressed mullet roe

praire *nf* clam

pralin *nm* praline

praline *nf* praline; sugared almond

praliné *nm* praline ice-cream

pré-salé *nm* salt meadow sheep, lamb, near-the-sea sheep

précoce *a* early-fruiting; (of cabbage) spring greens

précuit *a* pre-cooked

premier (ière) *a* prime; **~ cru** (of wine) first growth (locally determined quality designation)

prendre *vi* (of jelly &c) to set

préparation *nf* ready-made ingredients; preparation, preparing; (of table) laying

préparer *vt* to prepare, to dress

prépayé *a* pre-paid

présentation *nf* presentation, dressing

pressage *nm* (of cheese) pressing

presse *nm* (of fruit) squeezer; **~-orange** orange squeezer; **~-purée** potato masher

pressé *a* pressed, squeezed, crushed

pression (à) *nm* (of beer) draught; (of coffee) percolated

pressoir *nm* (of wine, food) press

présure *nf* rennet

prêt-à-manger *nm* fast food; ready-to-eat food

prêtre *nm* sand smelt

prévenir *vt* to warn; to book; to reserve

primeur *nf* new; early-harvested

primevère *nf* primrose

prince albert *a* (of beef) vegetable fondue/foie gras/ truffled and whole truffle-garnished

princesse *a* asparagus/truffle-garnished

printanière (à la) *a* spring-vegetables garnished

printemps *nm* spring; **rouleau de ~** spring roll

prix *nm* price; **~ fixe** table d'hôte, (of menu) set-price; **~ à débattre** as agreed, by arrangement

produit *nm* product, crop, offspring; **~ alimentaire** foodstuff

profiterole *nf* profiterole

progrès *nm* almond/hazelnut pastry-base

promotion *nf* special offer, sales promotion

propriétaire *nm/f* owner; (of wine) grower; **~ récoltant** (of wine) owner manager

prosciutto *nm* ham

protéine *nf* protein

provençal *a* Provençal; with

oil/garlic/tomato

province *nf* province, region, locality

provision *nf* deposit; **~s** provisions, supplies

prune *nf* plum; **~ de cythère** ambarella fruit; **~ de damas** damson

pruneau *nm* prune

prunelle *nf* sloe

psalliote (agaric) *nm* mushroom varieties: horse mushroom, field mushroom

pudding *nm* pudding, plum duff; **~ de pain** bread-and-butter pudding

puits *nm* well; **~ d' amour** jam or vanilla or praline flavoured cream-filled pastry

pulpe *nf* (of fruit/vegetables) flesh; pulp

punch *nm* punch

pur *a* (of water) sweet; (of whisky) malt; **le ~ brebis** ewe's milk cheese

purée *nf* mash, purée, thick cream; **~ de pois cassé** pease pudding; **saucisses à la ~** bangers and mash; (of potatoes) creamed, mashed, (of apples &c) snow

pyramide *nf* pyramid; goat cheese

Q

quadriller *vt* to square-pattern a food surface

qualité *nf* quality

quantité *nf* quantity

quartier *nm* (of beef/lamb) side

quarts-de-chaume *nm* Anjou sweet white wine

quasi *nm* cut of veal (rump)

quatre-épices *nm* 4 spices, mixed white pepper/nutmeg/ginger/cloves; all-spice

quatre-fruits *nm* 4 summer red fruits, strawberry/cherry/redcurrant/raspberry

quatre-quarts *nm* Madeira cake, pound cake

quenelle *nf* quenelle, fish/meat savoury paste

quetsche *nm* quetsch plum; quetsch plum liqueur

queue *nf* tail; (of fruit) stalk, stem

quiche *nf* quiche, savoury tart

quignon (cuignot) *nm* end crust of loaf

quincy *nm* Loire dry white wine

quinine *nf* quinine

quittance *nf* receipt

R

râble *nm* back, saddle

rachel *a* red wine-sauced beef-marrow-stuffed artichoke heart-garnished

racine *nf* root; **~ alimentaires** root crops

raclette *nf* cheese fondue; spatula

radis *nm* radish; **~ noir** horseradish

raffiner *vt* to refine

rafraîchir *vt* to cool, to chill; to chill with cold water

rafraîchissant *a* refreshing

rafraîchissements *nm* refreshments

ragoût *nm* (of meat) stew, ragout, meat/vegetable stew; ~ **grossier** mulligan stew, odds-and-ends stew

raidir *vt* to seal

raie *nf* skate, ray; ~ **bouclée** thornback ray

raifort *nm* horseradish

raiponce *nf* lamb's lettuce

raisiné *nm* grape jelly; sugarless jam

raisins *nm* grapes; ~ **secs** raisins; ~ **de smyrne** sultanas; ~ **de Corinthe** currants

raiteau *nm* small ray

raïto (raite) (rayte) *nm* tomato/onion/walnut/garlic spiced condiment

rajouter *vt* (of salt &c) to add

raki *nm* aniseed spirit

râle (des genêts) (d'eau) *nm* corncrake

rame (à) *nf* (of beans) runner

ramequin *nm* ramekin

ramier *nm* wood-pigeon

ramolli *a* soft

rance *a* rancid

rangement *nm* (of food/wine) storage

râpe *nf* (of cheese) grater

râper *vt* (of cheese) to grate

râpeur *nm* shredder, food-processor

râpure *nf* garlic oyster with herbs

rascasse *nf* scorpion fish

rassasier *vt* (of hunger) to satisfy

rassis (e) *a* (of bread) stale

rasteau *nm* Rhone wine

ratafia *nm* ratafia, small almond macaroon; almond liqueur (or certain fruit stone)

ratatouille *nf* stew of Mediterranean vegetables, ratatouille

ration *nf* ration, measured portion

ratte *nf* small yellow-skinned potato

rave *nf* rape

ravier *nm* hors d'oeuvre dish

ravigote *nf* dressing egg/vinaigrette

ravioles *nmpl* small ravioli

ravioli *nmpl* ravioli

rayer *vt* (of pastry) to decorate edge with fork/knife impressions

rayon *nm* (of fish) fin; **de** ~ (of honey) comb

rebibes *npl* cheese shavings

reblochon *nm* cow's milk cheese

reboucher *vt* to re-cork

récépissé *nm* receipt

réception *nf* reception

recette *nf* recipe; **livre de** ~**s** recipe book

réchaud *nm* stove

réchauffer *vt* to reheat

récoltant *nm* vineyard owner/manager

récolte *nf* (of fruit) crop, harvest; (of wine) vintage; **~ village** simple locally-classified wine; **~ villages** villages blended locally-classified wine

recommander *vt* to recommend

rectifier *vt* to rectify, to adjust

récu *nm* receipt

recuire *vt* to re-cook

récurer *vt* (of cleaning) to scour

réduction *nf* reduction, concentration, thickening

réduire *vt* to reduce, to boil down

réforme *a* (of sauce) Reform: espagnole sauce with gherkin/mushroom/truffle/hard-boiled egg white

réfrigérateur *nm* fridge

refroidir *vt* to cool

régal *nm* treat

régalec *nm* sea fish: ribbon-fish, oar-fish, 'king of the herrings'

régaler *vt* to regale, to treat to a feast

régence *a* very richly and variously garnished

régime *nm* diet; (of bananas) bunch

régler *vt* (of the bill) to settle-up

réglisse *nf* liquorice (licorice)

régnié *nm* beaujolais cru

reine *nf* queen; **~ de benotte** potato variety; **~-claude** greengage; **~ de saba** chocolate custard cake; **à la ~** sauced chicken-inclusive

reinette *nf* (of apple variety) cox

réjane *a* (of meat) potato/ spinach/artichoke/bone-marrow-garnished

relevé (e) *a* spicy; **sauce rouge ~e** russian dressing

relever *vt* to season, to spice

reliefs *nmpl* left-overs

remboursement *nm* reimbursement, rebate

remise *nf* discount

rémois *a* from Rheims

remontant *nm* (of drink) pick-me-up, bracer, tonic

remonter *vt* (of sauce) to reconstitute

rémora rayé *nm* sea fish: shark-sucker

remoudou *nm* soft cow's milk cheese

remouer *vt* to stir; (of salad) to toss

rémoulade *nf* dressing with herbs and mustard; mayonnaise with herbs/capers

remplir *vt* to fill

renaissance (à la) *a* vegetable-garnished

renard de mer *nm* thresher shark, fox shark

rendez-vous *nm* rendez-vous; meeting place

renne *nm* reindeer

renseignement *nm* information

renverser *vt* to spill

répandre *vt* to spill

repas *nm* meal

repasser *vt* (of knife) to sharpen

repasseur *nm* knife-sharpener

répertoire *nm* repertoire

reposant *a* relaxing

requin *nm* shark

réservation *nf* reservation

réserve *nf* (of wine) quality

réserver *vt* to reserve, to keep, to book; (of food) to set aside

résiné *a* (of wine) retsina, resinous white wine

restaurant *nm* restaurant; **~ libre-service** self-service restaurant; **~ rapide** fast-food restaurant

restaurateur (trice) *nm/f* restaurateur

restauration *nf* catering, catering trade

restes *nmpl* scraps, scrapings

rétamer *vt* (of pans) to re-tin, to re-line

retourner *vt* (of egg) to turn over

reuilly *nm* Loire wine

revenu *a* browned

revêtement *nm* (of saucepan) coating

rez-de-chaussée *nm* ground-floor

Rhin *nm* (of wine) hock

rhubarbe *nf* rhubarb

rhum *nm* rum

riche *a* rich; **(à la ~)** truffle-inclusive

richelieu *a* (of meat) tomato/mushroom/braised lettuce/potato-garnished; (of sole) truffle/parsley butter-garnished; (of cake) maraschino-almond sponge

ricotta (ricotte) *nf* ricotta, cow, ewe or goat soft white cheese

riesling *nm* Riesling, dry white wine

rifaut *nm* radish

rigotte (de condrieu) (de pélussin) *nf* (each) soft goat cheese

rillettes *nfpl* rillettes, chitterlings, potted pork or goose meat

rillons (rillots) (rillauds) (grillons) *nmpl* residue from rendered pork fat; caramel-browned pork shoulder or belly

rince-doigts *nm* finger-bowl

rincette *nf* rincer of brandy in still-warm coffee cup; post-prandial spirits

riolé *a* hatched with pastry strips

ripaille *nm* Haute-Savoie white wine; *nf* abundant feast

ris *nm* (of calf or lamb) sweetbread

risotto *nm* risotto, creamy stock-simmered rice

rissole *nf* rissole, fried ball of meat/fish with breadcrumbs

rissolée (couenne) *a* crackling; (of potato) fried

rissoler *vt* to brown

rivesaltes *nm* Roussillon red or white wine

rivière *nf* river

riz *nm* rice; **~ à grains ronds** pudding rice

robe des champs *(or* **de chambre)** *nf* (of potato) jacket

robe *nf* skin, husk; (of wine) colour

Robert *a* (of sauce) Robert, white wine/onion/mustard piquant sauced

roboratif (ive) *a* (of alcohol) stimulating

rocamadour *nm* goat cheese

rocambeau *a* potato/carrot/lettuce/cauliflower-garnished

rocambole *nf* garlic variety

roche *nf* (of fish) rock

rocher *nm* rock cake, biscuit

rocroi *nm* cow's milk cheese

rognon *nm* kidney

rognonade *nf* roast loin of veal kidneys-inclusive

rohan (à la) *a* supreme-sauced cock's kidney-tart and foie gras/truffle/artichoke heart-garnished

rollmops *nm* rollmop, uncooked pickled herring

rollot *nm* cow's milk cheese

romaine *a* (of lettuce) cos, romaine; **à la ~** (of sauce) sweet and sour vine-fruited/pine kernel-ed; (of gnocci) semolina/cheese-inclusive

romanesco *nm* cauliflower variety

romanov *a* potato/cucumber-inclusive; mushroom/celeriac/horseradish/velouté-garnished; (of strawberries) curaçao-ed with whipped cream

romarin *nm* rosemary

rombosse *nf* apple tart

rombou *nm* Mediterranean flat fish

romsteck (rumsteck) *nm* rump-steak

roncal *nm* ewe's milk cheese

ronce *nf* wild blackberry

rond *nm* slice; **~ de serviette** napkin ring

rondelle *nf* slice

ronger *vi* to gnaw

roquefort *nm* ewe's milk blue cheese

rosace *nf* rosette

rosbif *nm* roast-beef

rosé *a* pink, rosé; **~ des riceys** Aube rosé wine

rosette *nf* pork sausage

rosier (fruit de) *nm* hip

Rossini *a* demi-glaced foie gras/truffle-containing

rotengle *nm* freshwater fish: roach; rudd

rothomago *a* (of fried eggs) ham/chipolata/tomato sauce-garnished

Rothschild *a* pastry cream soufflé/crystallised fruit/liqueured

rôti *nm* roast, joint

rôtie *nf* toast; garnished toast

rotir *vt* to roast

rôtisserie *nf* grill, rotisserie, griddle

rôtissoire *nf* rotisserie; spit

rouelle *nf* (of calf's leg) slice

rouennais *a* from Rouen; (of sauce) strong red-wine/duck-liver/stock/buttered

rouffe impérial *nm* sea fish: black-fish variety

rougail *nm* highly-spiced seasoning

rouge *a* red; red wine

rouget *nm* ~ **barbet** red mullet; ~ **grondin** gurnard

rouille *nf* (of fish) spicy sauce

roulade *nf* stuffed and rolled ingredient

roulante *a* (of table) trolley

roulé *nm* roll; *a* rolled

rouleau *nm* roll; ~ **de printemps** spring roll; ~ **à pâtisserie** rolling-pin

rouler *vt* to roll up

roulette *nf* wheeled pastry-cutter

roussanne *nm* white grape variety

rousseau *nm* red sea bream

roussette *nf* rock salmon, dog-fish, bull huss; ~ **de savoie** Savoie white wine

roussir (faire) *vt* (of sauce) to brown

roux *nm* roux, thickening, soft butter/flour liaison; **sucre ~** demerara

royale *nf* (of soup) egg/consommé diced custard garnish

royale (à la) *nf* royale; savoury custard; (of soup) garnished royale; (of fish) mousseline sauced quenelles/mushroom/oyster/truffle; (of poultry) quenelles/mushroom-garnished; (of hare) richly stewed

rubens *a* white-wine brunoise madeira/egg-yolk/anchovy-sauced

ruche *nf* beehive

rue *nf* rue

ruifard *nm* chartreuse-flavoured pear or apple or quince pie

rully *nm* red or white burgundy

ruminant *a/nm* cud-chewing animal, ruminant

russe *a* (of salad) russian, including beetroot/sour-cream/mayonnaise; ~ **d'Oloron** Oloron gateau

russule *nf* mushroom russula variety: green cracking russula

rutabaga *nm* rutabaga, swede

S

sabayon *nm* zabaglione, syllabub, whipped egg yolks with sugar and wine

sablé *nm* shortbread; shortbread cake

sabler *vt* to bring to friable state

sablier *nm* egg-timer

sabre noir *nm* sea fish: scabbard-fish

saccharine *nf* saccharin

sacristain *nm* small twisted pastry stick

safrané *a* with saffron

sagan *a* mushroom-sauced/risotto/truffle/calf's brain-garnished

sagarno *nm* Basque apple wine

sagou *nm* sago

saignant *a* rare, underdone

saindoux *nm* pork fat, lard

saingorlon *nm* cow's milk cheese

saint-amour *nm* beaujolais wine

saint-aubin *nm* Beaune wine

saint-félicien *nm* soft cow's milk cheese

saint-florentin *nm* kirsch fruit-topped cream sponge cake; cow's milk cream cheese

saint-germain *a* peas-containing; (of fish) béarnaise-sauced breadcrumbs-covered

saint-honoré *nm* cream patisserie

saint-hubert *a* game-associated

saint-joseph *nm* Rhone red or white wine

saint-julien *nm* claret

saint-laurent *nm* red wine grape variety

saint-malo *nm* shallot-ed fish white sauce

saint-mandé *a* peas/beans/potato-garnished

saint-marcellin *nm* cow's milk cheese

saint-nectaire *nm* cow's milk cheese

saint-nicolas *nm* Touraine wine

saint-paulin *nm* cow's milk cheese

saint-péray *nm* Rhone white wine

saint-pierre *nm* dory, John Dory, St Peter's fish

saint-raphaël *nm* fortified wine

saint-romain *nm* Beaune wine

saint-saëns *a* (of poultry) foie gras fritters/truffle/cock's kidney/asparagus/supreme-sauced garnished

saint-véran *nm* white bergundy

sainte-alliance (à la) *a* foie gras/truffled

sainte-croix-du-mont *nm* bordeaux sweet white wine

sainte-menehould *a* mustarded/breadcrumbed

sainte-maure *nm* goat cheese

saisir *vt* to seal

saison *nf* season

saké *nm* sake, rice wine

salade *nf* lettuce, salad, endive; ~ **composée** mixed salad; ~ **de fruits** fruit salad/cocktail; ~ **russe** mayonnaised mixed vegetables

saladier *nm* salad bowl

saladine *nf* small salad

salamandre *nf* (of cooking) salamander, slow cooker, old grill

salami *nm* salami

salammbô *nm* chocolate-topped kirsch creamed patisserie

salé *a* salted, savoury

salée *nf* sugared creamed patisserie

salep *nm* starch

saler *vt* to cure

salers *nm* hard cow's milk cheese

salicorne *nf* glasswort

salière *nf* salt-cellar

salle *nf* room; ~ **à manger**

dining-room; **~ de bain** bathroom; **petite ~ à manger** breakfast-room; **~ de restaurant** restaurant dining-room

salmigondis *nm* hotchpotch

salmis *nm* salmi, wine stew

salmonelle *nf* salmonella

salpêtre *nm* saltpetre

salpicon *nm* salpicon; brown or white-sauced shredded chicken/ham/game or mushroom

salsepareille *nf* (of drink) sarsaparilla, sassafras-flavoured fizzy drink

salsifis *nm* salsify, vegetable 'oyster of the garden'

samaritaine (à la) *a* braised lettuce/rice/potato-garnished

sambuca *nf* sambuca aniseed liqueur

sancerre *nm* Loire *(usu)* white wine

sandre *nm* pikeperch

sandwich *nm* sandwich; butty

sang *nm* blood

sanglier *nm* wild boar

sangria *nf* sangria, red wine/lemonade/fruit drink

sanguin (e) *a* (of orange) blood

sanitaire *a* clean

santé *nf* **bonne ~** cheers! Your health!; sorrel/chervil soup

sapin *nm* fir

sar *nm* sea fish: sea bream

sarcelle *nf* teal, small wild duck

sardine *nf* sardine; **~ arc-en-ciel** *nf* sea fish: herring variety

sardinelle *nf* Mediterranean herring family sea fish

sarrasin *nm* buckwheat

sarriette *nf* savory, sage-like herb

sassenage *nm* blue cheese

satsuma *nf* satsuma

sauce *nf* sauce, gravy; **~ grand veneur** redcurrant/cream/vinegar/stock game-sauce

saucer *vt* (of bread) to dunk; to mop the plate

saucière *nf* gravyboat, sauceboat

saucisse *nf* sausage

saucisson *nm* large thick sausage; (of loaf) cylindrical

sauge *nf* sage

saumon *nm* salmon; **~ fumé** smoked salmon, lox; **~ de fontaine** American brook trout

saumonette *nf* shark sea fish: nurse hound

saumure *nf* brine, pickle

saupe *nf* sea fish: bream

saupoudrage *nm* dredging, powdering, sprinkling

saupoudrer *vt* to dredge, to powder, to sprinkle

saupoudreuse *nf* sugar caster

saupiquet *nm* spicey stew

saur (hareng) *a* kipper

saurel *nf* scad, horse mackerel

sauté *a* tossed, sauté, shallow fried; *nm* sauté

sauterelle *nf* grasshopper, locust

sauternes *nm* bordeaux white

wine

sauteuse *nf* frying-pan

sautoir *nm* high-sided frying-pan

sauvage *a* wild, feral

sauvageon *nm/f* wild fruit *esp* apple

sauvagine *nf* wildfowl

sauvennières *nm* Loire white wine

sauver *vt* (of meat) to smoke, to cure

sauvignon blanc *nm* Loire/ Bordeaux white grape variety

sauvissage *nm* (of meat) smoking, curing

savagnin *nm* white wine grape variety

savarin *nm* savarin, nut/fruit-filled cake

saveur *nf* flavour

Savoie *nf* Savoy; **biscuit de ~** sponge cake

savon *nm* soap; **~ de Marseille** kitchen soap

savourer *vt* to taste, to savour

savoyarde (à la) *a* savoyarde, with egg/milk/potato/gruyère

scampi *nmpl* scampi

scarole *nf* endive variety

schnaps *nm* schnapps

scone *nm* scone

scorpène *nf* scorpion fish

screwdriver *nm* orange/vodka cocktail

seau *nm* bucket; **~ à glace** ice-bucket

sébaste *nm* sea fish: red-fish, norway haddock, bluemouth, scorpion fish variety

sec (sèche) *a* dry; (of grapes) raisin

sèche *nf* cumin/lardons cake

sécher *vt* to cure, to dry, to desiccate

secouer *vt* (of salad) to shake

seelac *nm* smoked black pollack, hake

seiche *nf* cuttlefish

seigle *nm* (of bread) rye; **~ noir** pumpernickel; **pain de ~** black bread

séjour *nm* stay, sojourn

sel *nm* salt; **~ fin** table salt; **~ gemme** rock salt; **~ marin** sea-salt

sélar *nm* sea fish: scad variety

selle *nf* saddle

selle-sur-cher *nm* soft goat cheese

seltz (eau de) *nf* soda water, seltzer

sémillon *nm* sweet Bordeaux grape variety

semoule *nf* semolina

senteur *nf* smell, scent

sentir *vt* to smell

séparer (se) *vi* (of liquids) to separate

sérac *nm* cow's milk cheese

séré *nm* white cheese

serge (à la) *a* breadcrumbs/ mushroom/truffle/artichoke/ ham-garnished

série *nf* (of pans &c) set

seringue *nf* syringe

sériole *nf* sea fish: amberjack

serpent *nm* snake

serpolet *nm* mother-of-thyme

serran *nm* sea fish: sea-perch variety

serran-chevrette *nm* sea fish: comber

serrano *nm* dry ham

serrée *a* (of sauce) thick

serveur (euse) *nm/f* waiter/ waitress, bartender

service *nm* service; ~ **de table** dinner service; ~ **compris** tip included

serviette *nf* napkin, serviette; **rond de** ~ napkin-ring; **à la** ~ *a* placed on napkin

servir *vt* to serve; to ladle out

sésame *nm* sesame

séteau *nm* sole

sètoise (à la) *a* (of fish) mayonnaised

sève *nf* sap

seyssel *nm* savoie white wine

seyval blanc *nm* white wine grape variety

shadine ronde *nf* sea fish: herring variety

shaker *nm* (of cocktails) shaker

sharon *nm* sharon-fruit (charon-fruit)

sherry *nm* sherry

shiitake *nm* shiitake mushroom

shiraz *nm* wine grape variety

sicilienne (à la) *a* stuffed tomato/ rice/potato-garnished

side-car *nm* lemon/brandy/ cointreau cocktail

siffleur *a* (of duck) widgeon (wigeon)

siki *nm* shagreen shark

silure glane *nm* catfish

singapour *nm* large fruit-filled decorated sponge cake

singe *nm* monkey

singer *vt* to sprinkle with flour

siphon *nm* (of soda) syphon (siphon)

sirene *nm* ewe's milk cheese

sirop *nm* syrup; ~ **d'églantine** rosehip syrup; ~ **d'orgeat** barleywater, orgeat

slivovica *nf* slivovitz, plum brandy

sloke *nm* sloke, sea spinach

smitane *nf* smetana, sour cream

smoking *nm* dinner-jacket

smorgasbord (smörgåsbord) *nm* smorgasbord, scandinavian canapés; black bread open sandwich

soave *nm* Italian white wine

sobre *a* frugal, abstemious

sobronade *nf* pork or ham-garnished vegetable soup

socca *nf* chickpea flour

socle *nm* bread base

soda *nm* fizzy drink; **whisky** ~ whisky and soda

soif *nf* thirst; **vin de** ~ light thirst-quenching wine

soir *nm* evening

soirée *nf* reception, party

soissons *nmpl* dwarf beans

soja (soya) *nm* soya; **fromage de** ~ bean curd; **germes de** ~ beanshoots; **graine de** ~ soyabean; **farine de ~** soya flour

sole *nf* sole

solenette *nf* flat sea-fish: solenette

solferino *nf* buttery tomato sauce

solide *a* solid

soliflore *nm* single-flower vase

solilemme (solimem) *nm* rich brioche

solognote (à la) *a* (of duck) pot-roasted minced with breadcrumbs

soluble *a* (of coffee) instant

sommelier *nm* wine waiter

son *nm* bran

sorbais *nm* cow's milk cheese

sorbe *nf* rowan-berry

sorbet *nm* sorbet, water ice, sherbet; between courses palate-refreshing agent

sorbetière *nf* sorbet-maker; ice-cream maker

sorgho *nm* sorghum

sortie *nf* exit; **~ de secours** fire exit

sot-l'y-laisse *nm* (of poultry) oyster

sou-fassum *nm* stewed meat/rice/vegetable-stuffed cabbage

soubise *nf* soubise, béchamel onion-purée sauce

souchet (suchet) *nm* vegetable/white-wine/fish-stock sauce

souci *nm* marigold

soude *nf* soda; **bicarbonate de ~** bicarbonate of soda

soufflé *nm* soufflé

souffler *vt* (of candle) blow out, extinguish

soûl *a* plastered, drunk

soumaintrain *nm* cow's milk cheese

soupçon *nm* drop, tiny amount, hint

soupe *nf* soup; **~ populaire** soup kitchen

souper *nm* supper

soupière *nf* soup tureen

source *nf* (of water) spring

sourdon *nm* cockle

souris *nf* (of meat) knuckle; **~ de mer** sea fish: pogge

sous-noix *nf* (of veal) leg

soutirage *nm* (of wine) decanting

souvarova *a* (of game/poultry) foie gras/truffle-stuffed

spaghetti *nmpl* spaghetti

sparaillon *nm* sea fish: bream variety

spätlese *nm* german late-harvested high-quality white wine category

spatule *nf* spatula; slice

spätzle (spätzele) (spetzli) *nf* spätzle; dumpling

spécialité *nf* speciality

spectacle *nm* floor-show, cabaret

spéculos *nm* patisserie of butter/flour/cinnamon/egg/cloves

spiral *a* spiral

spiritueux *nmpl* spirits

spirlin *nm* freshwater fish: alburnoides bipunctatus: schneider fish

spoom *nm* spoom, light sorbet

sprat (esprot) (sprot) *nm* sprat, brisling

squale *nm* shark

stanley *a* curry/onion-including

steak *nm* steak

stériliser *vt* to sterilise

sterlet *nm* sea fish: sturgeon

steward *nm* (of ship) steward

stimuler *vt* (of appetite) to whet

stoba *nm* goat/olive stew

stockfisch *nm* stockfish, dried cod

stoemp *nm* vegetable/potato mash

stout *nm* stout

strasbourg *nf* (of sausage) beef

strasbourgeoise (à la) *a* sauerkraut/bacon/foie gras-garnished; (of consommé) red cabbage/sausage/horse-radish/juniper berry-including

strate *nf* layer

streusel *nm* vanilla-creamed almond-ed brioche

stroganov *a* (of beef) strogonoff; onion/mushroom-garnished cream-sauced

strophaire à anneau rugueux *nf* mushroom type: rozites caperata

strudel *nm* thin filled pastry case

subric *nm* savoury butter-fried croquette hors d'oeuvre (as dessert if sweet)

substantiel (elle) *a* (of meal) copious, substantial, solid

suc *nm* juice

succédané *nm* (of milk) substitute

succès *nf* praline butter-creamed almond meringue

succharose *nf* sucrose

succulent *a* succulent

sucer *vt* to suck; **bonbon à ~** boiled sweet

sucette *nf* lollipop

suchet *a* (of scalloped shellfish) white wine-cooked or mornay-sauce accompanied

sucrant *a* sweetening

sucrase *nf* sucrase

sucre *nm* sugar: **~ candi** candy; **~ de canne** cane; **~ cristallisé** granulated; **~ d'orge** barley sugar; **~ en poudre** caster; **~ en pain** sugarloaf; **~ glace** icing; **~ roux (brun)** demerara, brown sugar; **~ semoule** powder, caster

sucré *a* sweet, sweetened; **non-~** savoury

sucrer *vt* to sugar, to sweeten

sucrerie *nf* sweetmeat, confection

sucrier *nm* sugar bowl

suédoise *nf* cream-covered fruit jelly; **à la ~** *a* herb vinaigretted vegetable/fruit/mushroom/cheese/(shell)fish-garnished

suer *vi* to sweat

suif *nm* (of mutton) suet

sulfurisé *a* (of paper) greaseproof

sultane (à la) *a* pistachio nut-including

sumac *nm* sumac (sumach)
sundae *nm* sundae
supion *nm* small cuttlefish
supplément *nm* extra
suprême *nm* supreme, the best; stock/cream/egg-yolk sauce; (of fowl) breast/wing
surprise (en) *nf* (of dish) surprise, of unexpectedly different flavour/constitution
sur *a* sour, acid, bitter
surabondance *nf* glut
surbooking *nm* double-booking
surchoix *a* (of meat) top quality, prime
surcoût *nm* extra cost
sureau *nm* elder
suret (ette) *a* (of taste) sharp, tart
surgelé *a* deep-frozen
surtout *nm* table decorative centrepiece
sushi *nm* sushi, cold vinegar-ed rice balls of vegetable/egg/raw seafood
suzette *nf* (of crêpe) flambé-ed orange-liqueur pancake
syrop *nm* syrup

T

tabac *nm* tobacco
table *nf* table; **~ d'honneur** high table; **~ d'hôte** communal table; **~ roulante** trolley; **se mettre à ~** to sit down; **mettre la ~** to lay the table; **vin de ~** basic every-day wine

tableau *nm* blackboard, *(US)* chalkboard
tablette *nf* (of chocolate) bar, block, slab
tablier *nm* apron; **~ de sapeur** breaded deep-fried tripe
taboulé *nm* tabbouleh, burghul/parsley/onion/mint, lemon juice/oil/spices-salad.
tacaud *nf* bib fish, whiting pout, pouting, gadidae-family fish
tache *nf* (of fruit) spot, blemish
tafia *nm* poor-quality rum
tagine (tajine) *nm* earthenware pot, stew
tagliatelles *nfpl* tagliatelli, thin strips of pasta
tagor *nm* tangerine/orange cross
tahitienne (à la) *a* (of marinated raw fish) tomato/coconut-garnished
taillé *a* cut, trimmed; *nm* pork pastry
taillon *nm* (of potato) round slice
tajine (tagine) *nm* earthenware pot, stew
taler (se) *vi* (of fruit) to bruise
talmouse *nf* cheesed béchamel pastry
talon *nm* tail-end cut of meat, remainder, residue; upper shoulder; (of cheese/bread) heel, crust, discarded-part
tamarillo *nm* tamarillo fruit
tamarin *nm* tamarind
tamis *nm* (for solids) sieve, sifter
tamiser *vt* to sieve
tamponner *vt* (of butter) to dab

with

tanche *nf* river fish: tench

tangelo *nm* tangelo, grapefruit/ tangerine cross

tangerine *nf* tangerine

tanin *nm* tannin

tannat *nm* red grape variety

tapenade *nf* tapenade, olive/ anchovy/caper hors d'oeuvre

tapioca *nm* tapioca

tarama *nm* tarama (taramasalata), fish roe pâté

tarator *nf* cucumber/nut/yoghourt salad

tardive *a* (of grape harvest) late

targeur *nm* flat sea fish: topknot

tarif *nm* tariff

taro *nm* taro tuber

tarpon *nm* tarpon sea fish

tartare *a* tartar sauce, mayonnaise with hard boiled egg yolks/herbs/capers/ gherkins

tarte *nf* tart, flan

tartelette *nf* tartlet, small tart

tartibas *nf* grape pancakes

tartine *nf* bread and butter

tartiner (de) *vt* (of bread) to spread

tas *nm* heap, pile, load, lashing(s)

tasse *nf* cup, cupful

tassergal *nm* sea fish: pomatomus saltator, bluefish

tasteviné *a* (of burgundy) tastings-passed

tâte-vin *nm* wine-taster, tastevin (taste-vin)

tatin *nf* caramelised apple tart

tatou *nm* armadillo

taupe *nf* shark variety: porbeagle

tavel *nm* Rhone rosé wine

tavelure *nf* (of fruit) spot, blemish

taverne *nf* tavern, inn, brasserie

taxi *nm* taxi, cab

tchorba *nf* chicken/offal soup

télécopieur *nm* fax

téléphone *nm* telephone

télétexte *nm* teletext

telfairia *nm* telfairia gourd

telline *nf* clam variety: telline

tempérance *nf* temperance

tempérant *a* abstinent, temperate

température *nf* temperature

tende-de-tranche *nm* top of thigh

tendineux (euse) *a* (of meat) stringy

tendre *a* tender

tendron *nm* tendron, flank breast

teneur *nf* (of alcohol) proof

tentacule *nm* tentacle, feeler

tenter *vt* to tempt

tequila *nf* agave spirit

terminer *vt* (of meal) to finish

terre *nf* sea fish: sting ray

terre cuite *nf* terracotta

terrine *nf* terrine, pâté; earthenware pot

terroir *nm* soil; (of taste) earthyness

tête *nf* head; (of cheese) headcheese; **~ marbrée** jellied pickled pig's head; **~ pressée** brawn; jellied loaf of half pig's head/ear/2 trotters; **~ de moine** cow's milk cheese

tétine *nf* udder

tétras *nm* capercailzie, capercaillie, large grouse

tétras-lyre *nm* blackcock

texture *nf* texture

tfina *nm* dafina, spicy chick pea/ beef/egg/potato ragout

thai *a* Thai

thazard *nm* sea fish: frigate mackerel, plain bonito

thé *nm* tea

théière *nf* teapot

thermidor *a* (of lobster) thermidor; mustard/bercy sauce-cooked au gratin/mornay sauce-served

thermomètre *nm* thermometer

thermos *nm* vacuum flask

thermostat *nm* gas mark

thon *nm* tunny, tuna fish; **~ blanc** longfin; **~ rouge** bluefin

thonine *nf* sea fish: little tunny, false albacore

thym *nm* thyme

tian *nm* vegetable gratin; shallow earthenware dish

tiède *a* warm, lukewarm, tepid

tienne: à (la) *pos pro (familiar)* your health! cheers!

tige *nf* stalk

tilleul *nm* lime tree

tilsit *nm* cow's milk cheese

timbale *nf* timbale, meat/fish creamed into mould; mug

tiramisu *nm* tiramisu, chocolate/ mascarpone cheese-covered

coffee/brandy-soaked sponge

tire-bouchon *nm* corkscrew

tire-larigot (à) *a* over-the-top, well-oiled

tirer *vt* (of cork) to extract

tisane *nf* herb tea

tivoli *a* suprême-sauced asparagus/mushroom/ cockscomb/kidney-garnished

toast *nm* (of welcome) verbal well-wishing, toast; (of bread) toast, grilled sliced bread; **~ au fromage** Welsh rabbit (rarebit)

tofu *nm* tofu, bean curd

toilette *nf* toilet; (of pork) intestine

tokay *nm* sweet hungarian white wine

tom-pouce *nm* nut/coffee cream pastry sandwich

tomate *nm* tomato; **~-cerise** *nf* cherry tomato; aniseed/ grenadine aperitif

tombe *nf* pearl gurnard fish

tomber *vi* (of mayonnaise) to curdle, to separate; to cook slowly in own juice; **~ à glace** to reduce

tomme *nm* cow/goat/ewe cheeses

tonic *nm* tonic water

tonique *a* (of wine &c) tonic, fortifying

tonka *nm* tonka bean

tonkinois *nm* almond/praline cake; almond/nougatine petit four

tonneau *nm* barrel, butt

tonnelet *nm* small barrel, keg

topinambour *nm* Jerusalem artichoke

toque *nf* toque, chef's hat

torchon *nm* teacloth, drying-up cloth

torrée *nf* sausage cooked in ashes; the ensuing meal

torréfié *a* (of coffee &c) roasted

torteil (torteau) *nm* aniseed brioche

tortellini *nm* stuffed pasta

tortillon *nm* petit four of twisted puff pastry

tortue (en) *a* (of calf's head) simmered served on croûtons

tortue d'eau douce *nf* terrapin, small tidal-water tortoise

tortue marine *nf* turtle

toscane (à la) *a* parmesan/ham-including; (of macaroni) truffle/foie gras-sauced

toulousaine (à la) *a* south-west france-influenced

toupin *nm* earthenware pot; cow's milk cheese

toupinel *a* (of poached egg) mornay-sauced in baked potato

tourangelle (à la) *a* (of meat) french and flageolet bean-garnished; (of egg) bean-purée/cream sauced on tartlet

tourbe *nf* peat

tourbeux *a* peaty

tourer *vt* (of pastry) to fold and roll

tourin *nm* onion soup

touristique *a* tourist; **menu ~** economy menu, set menu

tourné *a* (of milk) sour

tournebroche *nm* spit

tournedos *nm* heart of fillet of meat thick cut, tournedos

tourner *vi* (of fruit/milk) to turn, to go off; *vt* (of salad) to toss; (of liquid) to stir

tournesol *nm* sunflower

touron *nm* almond/pistachio/orange essence/cream petit four

tourte *nf* pie; **~ de bakewell** Bakewell tart

tourteau *nm* crab; **~ fromagé** brandied goat cheese pastry

tourterelle *nf* dove

tourtière *nf* meat pâté in pastry-case; pie-dish

tourtillon *nm* citron-peel cake

toute-épice *nf* nigella

traire *vt* (of cows) to milk

trait *nm* (of cocktail) touch of alcohol

traiteur *nm* caterer

traminer *nm* white wine grape variety

tranche *nf* slice, rasher, steak; **~ grasse** silverside

tranchelard *nm* long-bladed knife

tranchoir *nm* platter; chopper

tranquille *a* (of wine) still; (of location) quiet, tranquil

transvaser *vt* to decant

trappiste *nf* beer; cow's milk cheese

travailler *vt* (of pastry dough) to

knead; to work-in

travers *nm* spare rib

trempé *a* soaked

tremper *vt* to soak

trempette *nf* dunking-bread; dunking-sugar

trenchant *a* (of knife) sharp; *nm* sharpness

trévise *nf* radicchio lettuce

tricholome *nm* mushroom varieties: tricholoma varieties: firwood agaric, dingy agaric; **~ sinistre** common field blewit (blue-leg)

tricorne *nm* goat cheese

trinquer à *vi* to chink glasses to

tripe (à la) *a* (of hard-boiled egg) with sweated onion/béchamel sauce

triperie *nf* tripe-shop produce; offal

tripes *nfpl* tripe, chitterlings

triple-sec *nm* orange liqueur

tripous (tripoux) *nmpl* sheep's offal/feet dish

trognon *nm* core, stalk

trompette-des-morts *nf* horn of plenty mushroom, craterelle, trumpet of death *(edible nevertheless! ed)*

tronçon *nm* slice, section; medallion

tropézienne *a* from St Tropez; rum cream brioche

troquet *nm* boozer, drinking establishment

trou-normand *nm* mid-prandial eau-de-vie

trouble *a* (of wine) cloudy

trousser *vt* (of poultry) to truss; to position before trussing

trouville *a* (of lobster) mornay-sauced au gratin mixed with sauced mushroom/oyster/mussels/truffle

truelle *nf* (of fish) fish-slice

truffe *nf* truffle; **~ en chocolat** chocolate truffle

truffer *vt* (of dish) to truffle

truie *nf* (of pig) sow

truite *nf* trout; **~ arc en ciel** rainbow trout; **~ de mer** seatrout; **~ saumonée** salmon trout

tsarine (à la) *a* (of fish/meat) cucumber-including; Russia-inspired

tubercule *nm* tuber

tuile *nf* sweet biscuit

tulipe *nf* tulip; delicate shaped-biscuit

turban *nm* turban

turbigo *a* (of kidneys) white wine-sauced with mushroom/chipolatas

turbot *nm* sea fish: turbot

turinois *nm* chestnut/chocolate/kirsch uncooked cake

turque (à la) *a* Turkey-influenced; rice-including

tusillage *nm* coltsfoot

tutti-frutti *a* all-fruit, mixed fruit in various forms

tyrolienne (à la) *a* tomato fondue/fried onion-garnished; (of sauce) oil-based tomato béarnaise

U

ugni blanc *nm* south-west France grape variety
unilatéral (ale) *a* on one side
ustensile *nm* utensil

V

vacance *nf* holiday
vache *nf* cow
vacherin *nm* vacherin, meringue/cream/fruit/ice cream dessert; cow's milk cheese
vachette *nf* calf
vacqueyras *nm* Rhone wine
vairon *nm* minnow
vaisselle *nf* crockery, tableware; **~(s)** dishes; **faire les ~(s)** *vt* to wash up
valançay *nf* goat cheese
valdiguié *nm* grape variety
valencienne (à la) *a* peppers/smoked ham-garnished
valenciennes (à la) *a* north of France-influenced
valise *nf* suitcase
vallée *nf* valley
valois *a* potato/artichoke/(olives)-garnished
vandoise *nf* dace
vanille *nf* vanilla
vanillé *a* vanilla-ed
vanneau *nm* lapwing; small coquille saint-jacques, queen scallop

vanner *vt* to stir until cold
vapeur *nf* steam; **à la ~** steamed
variante *nf* pickle
veau *nm* veal; **~ de mer** shark variety; **~ marin** seal
végétal *a* and *nm* vegetable, **cellulose ~** fibre
végétalien (ienne) *nm/f* vegan
végétarien (ienne) *nm/f* vegetarian
veille (de la) *nf* yesterday's; the day before's
veine *nf* cut of neck of beef
velours *nm* (of sauce) smooth
velouté *a* velouté, creamed, (of wine) mellow; *nm* soup
venaco *nm* soft goat or ewe's milk cheese
venaison *nf* venison
vendange *nm* grape harvest; **~ tardive** (of wine) late harvest
vendéen (enne) *a* from the Vendée
vendôme *nm* cow's milk cheese
Vendredi saint *nm* Good Friday; **brioche du ~** hot-cross bun
vénitienne (à la) *a* vénitienne-sauced; **sauce ~** tarragon-ed/vinegar-ed allemande sauce
ventadour *a* potato/artichoke purée/truffle/bone marrow-garnished
ventre *nm* belly, stomach
ventrèche *nf* streaky bacon
vénus *nm* venus clam
verdier *a* (of hard-boiled eggs) foie gras/onion/béchamel/parmesan-stuffed

verdure *nf* green salad; mixed green pot herbs

vergeoise *nf* soft brown sugar

vergus (verjus) *nm* verjuice, acid fruit liquor

vermicelle *nm* vermicelli, fine spaghetti; **potage au ~** noodle soup

vermouth *nm* vermouth; **gin-~** gin and it

vernis *nm* clam variety

vernon *a* artichoke heart/ asparagus/stuffed turnip/ mashed potato peas-stuffed/ apple-garnished

véronique *a* véronique, with white grape garnish; veronica

verrat *nm* male boar

verre *nm* glass; **~ à feu** ovenproof glass; **~ ballon** brandy balloon; **~ gradué** measuring jug; **~ perdu** (of bottles) disposable; **servi au ~** by the glass

verser *vt* to pour

verseuse *nf* coffee pot

vert *a* green, unripe, immature; **citron ~** (of fruit) lime; **~-cuit** almost raw; **~ pré** maître d'hôtel-sauced potato/ watercress liqueur-garnished

verveine *nf* (of tea, of liqueur) verbena

vesse-de-loup *nf* mushroom variety: puffball

vessie *nf* bladder

viande *nf* meat

vichy *a* (of water) Vichy; (of carrots) cooked in Vichy water

vichyssoise *a* Vichyssoise, creamy potato/leek soup

vide-pomme *nm* corer

videler *vt* to rim-pattern pastry manually

vider *vt* (of game birds, poultry) to draw

vieille *nf* sea fish: wrasse

vieillissement *nm* (of wine/ cheese) ageing

viennois *a* Viennese; (of coffee/ chocolate drink) with whipped cream

viennoise *a* (of veal) wiener schnitzel, escalope of veal

viennoiserie *nf* non-bread Vienna bakery products

vierge *a* (of oil) virgin, unrefined; (of sauce) basil/tomato/ coriander/lemon/olive oil

vieux (vieille) *a* old; (vieille) sea fish: wrasse; **~ boulogne** cow's milk cheese; **~ille vignes** 28-80 year old vines; high quality vines

vigne *nf* vine, vineyard

vigneau *nm* winkle

vigneron (onne) *nm/f* wine grower; **à la ~ne** *a* grapes/ autumn produce-inclusive

vignoble *nm* vineyard

vignot *nm* winkle

villageoise (à la) *a* white mushroom/onion-sauced

villages *nmpl* (of wine) best parts of region

villeroi *a* (of sauce) mushroom

allemande

vin *nm* wine; **~ de paille** wine made from grapes dried on straw mats

vinaigre *nm* vinegar; pickle

vinaigrette *nf* vinaigrette, oil/vinegar dressing, french dressing

vinaigrier *nm* vinegar-bottle

vinasse *nf* plonk

vincent *nf* herbs/hardboiled egg mayonnaise

viognier *nm* grape variety

violet *nm* violet shell-fish

violette *nf* violet flower

viroflay *a* (of dish) with-spinach

visitandine *nf* almond/egg-white cake

viticulture *nf* winegrowing

vivaneau *nm* red snapper

vive *nf* weever fish

voandzeia *nf* voandzeia bean

vodka *nf* vodka

voilé *a* draped with sugar threads

voilier *nm* sea fish: Atlantic sail-fish

voisinage *nm* neighbourhood

vol-au-vent *nm* puff pastry case holding fricassé chicken/fish

volaille *nf* poultry, fowl; **foie de ~** chicken liver

volatile *nm* fowl

volnay *nm* Beaune red wine

volonté (à) *nf* of your choice

volume *nm* bulk, roughage

volvaire *nf* mushroom variety: slimy volvar

vosne-romanée *nf* red burgundy wine

vôtre! (à (la)) your health! cheers!

vouvray *nm* white Loire wine

vue *nf* view

W

walewska (à la) *a* (of poached fish) lobster/truffle/mornay sauce-garnished

wapiti *nm* deer

waterzoï (waterzooï) *nm* (of boiled fish or chicken) crème fraiche/butter-garnished

whisky (Irish whiskey) *nm* whisky, scotch, bourbon; **~ au citron** whisky sour; **~ à l'eau** highball

winterthur *a* (of langouste) shrimp-sauced

X

xamango *nm* ham

xavier *nf* cream soup

xérès *nm* sherry

Y

yack (yak) *nm* yak

yaourt (yoghourt) *nm* yoghurt (yogurt)

Z

zakouski *nm* zakuska, russian

hors d'oeuvre
zébu *nm* zebu ox
zéphyr *a* of light consistency
zéro *a* (of champagne) bone dry
zeste *nm* zest
zingara *a* tomato/paprika-
  containing